For B. G.
Half Hope

ABOUT THE AUTHOR

Stacey Graham has spent a good part of the last twenty years as a ghost hunter sitting in dark attics waiting to poke the paranormal and see if it giggles. When not wrestling ghosts, she enjoys reading Jane Austen and writing zombie poetry, humor, and ghost stories. She is the author of *The Girls' Ghost Hunting Guide* and the *Zombie Tarot*, plus numerous short stories.

She lives outside of Washington, DC, with her husband, five daughters, and festive woodland creatures. Please visit her websites at staceyigraham.com and weeghosties .com, at Twitter @staceyigraham, and on Facebook at facebook.com/authorstaceygraham.

HAUNTED STUFF

DEMONIC DOLLS, SCREAMING SKULLS AND OTHER CREEPY COLLECTIBLES

STACEY GRAHAM

Llewellyn Publications
Woodbury, Minnesota

FIRST EDITION
Second Printing, 2016

Book design by Bob Gaul
Cover design by Percolator Graphic Design
Cover image: Shutterstock.com/147014423/©Jakub Krechowicz
Editing by Ed Day
Interior Images © Beth Bartlett, LaMishia Allen, Library of Congress,
          Lucy Cheung, Stacey Graham, and Theresa Apple

Llewellyn Publications is a registered trademark of Llewellyn Worldwide Ltd.

Library of Congress Cataloging-in-Publication Data
Graham, Stacey, 1968–
  Haunted stuff: demonic dolls, screaming skulls & other creepy
collectibles/Stacey Graham.—First Edition.
      pages cm
  Includes bibliographical references.
  ISBN 978-0-7387-3908-3
1. Ghosts. 2. Collectibles--Miscellanea. 3. Parapsychology. I. Title.
  BF1471.G73 2014
  133.1075—dc23
                    2014006068

Llewellyn Publications
A Division of Llewellyn Worldwide Ltd.
2143 Wooddale Drive
Woodbury, MN 55125-2989
www.llewellyn.com

Printed in the United States of America

Contents

Introduction   1

One: *How We Interpret Ghosts*   5

Two: *Demonic Dolls and Creepy Collectibles*   31

Three: *Restless Bones*   53

Four: *Haunted Housekeeping and Frightening Furniture*   79

Five: *Out of Pocket Experiences*   107

Six: *Spooky Seas*   133

Seven: *Betwixt and Between in Haunted Hotels*   155

Eight: Tinseltown   181

Nine: Jinxes   195

Conclusion   207

Appendix: How did our ancestors
   protect themselves from ghosts?   209

Acknowledgments   219

Bibliography   221

INTRODUCTION

Finding a one-of-a-kind antique doll in a garage sale is a great feeling, until you bring it home and it asks you for a glass of water. Haunted objects quietly invade our homes through auctions, yard sales, shady antique dealers, and the most insidious of all: grandmothers. Items inherited through the generational shifting of silverware may take on a darker side if a relative has attached herself to an oyster fork after her death.

What creates a haunted object? What saturates something that has no soul so that it carries with it the pain of a broken heart or the violence of a death? Call them cursed or call them blessed, these items frequently bump into our lives, creating phenomena that can't be explained by the cat. Haunted portraits, chairs that doom people to horrible deaths, or dolls that you thought only existed in bad movies—the mundane creates its own horror through the memories forced on it by former owners and passed on to new ones. You may think twice before hitting the next garage sale.

So how does an object become haunted? Is it likely that a ghost has wiggled its way between molecules and is embedded within the fibers of an object because it can't bear to be without it? Possibly. The first law of thermodynamics states that energy cannot be created nor destroyed—it can only be transferred—so one theory about what we call a "haunted object" is simply that energy is being deposited onto an item instead of it floating around the ether and popping up at inopportune times, such as on your way to the fridge at midnight. The energy leaves a residue that enables the object to present itself to people sensitive enough to pick up on its shenanigans in the way of movement, talking, feelings of doom—you get the picture. An item may also be used as an agent for the spirit to manipulate, such as a chair being thrown across a room, but does that mean the possesion is possessed, or merely in the right place at the wrong time?

Other objects such as roads, houses, and waterways may also be haunted through the transference of a great emotional experience. While we may tend to think of a haunted item as something we can keep in our pockets or hidden under the bed, these larger objects may be dipped in that same paranormal goo and have just as much of a story to tell as a haunted doll.

Why are the living drawn to ghost stories of haunted objects? We're curious. Not just about what happens after death but to discover the answers to the real mystery of *why* an object becomes haunted. Does every portrait have a backstory? Does every bed have a memory of those who slumbered? Why do some items manifest in paranormal activity while others don't make a peep? If it's any comfort, paranormal researchers are still watching and waiting to learn more about the interactions of the otherworld with the living. As we creep closer to the truth, however, we need to ask ourselves if we're comfortable with the answers we'll find. So keep that nightlight handy—just in case.

ONE

HOW WE INTERPRET GHOSTS

Not every spirit has the good manners to wait until we're prepared to receive them rationally. Unless we've been primed to expect something paranormal, the living tune out things such as ghosts, telemarketers, and infomercials. It's the mind's way of helping us to sort through the jumble of information that we're bombarded with daily and prioritize what's important. With ghosts, our brain is ready to rationalize what we're seeing into patterns that make sense, a phenomenon called pareidolia. It registers that a doll can't blink on its own, though when it happens, you may attribute it to a trick of the light or think that your imagination is interfering with common sense.

Chances are you've already encountered the paranormal. Those shadows that escape your vision as you turn your head or a faint smell that triggers a memory can make you wonder if something is a bit askew. As we learn to ignore the influence of ghosts, other more mundane things such as cable bills and needing new tires replace them. It's only when we relax and allow our senses to be off guard that we truly begin to see reality's fuzzy edges.

WHERE HAUNTED OBJECTS LURK

Ever find an object giving you the high sign from a crowded table at a flea market? Paranormal media such as books and television shows have helped collectors tune in to the vibrations haunted items are emitting with examples of what to look for: jewelry, toys, photographs, and even clothing. As ghostly treasure hunters, collectors are looking for items that speak to them—sometimes literally. If you're not in the market for a little paranormal rodeo, however, keep the following in mind and be wary of what may come home with that antique crib.

The following is a list of some places that commonly deal in items that may come with a phantom hitchhiker. While most sellers are unaware of a haunted past, they may be able to give you information about the piece itself.

Be sure to chat them up and take their business card in case you need help in your research later or want to return the item because of its activity.

Estate sales: That lonely-looking cookie jar may have been passed over for a reason. As homeowners die and their families are left with the painful chore of deciding what goes home in the back of their mini-van and what to leave behind, items with no senti-mental value (especially those not easily stored or transported) are often sold for others to enjoy. Larger furniture such as beds or mirrors are frequently for sale. As items that have a physical attachment to the former owners, such as the bed or a personal one, such as the mirror, these are great finds that may in-troduce the memories of a ghost into your new space.

Smaller items such as knick-knacks or kitchen gadgets can also launch paranormal activity. Aside from being a dust magnet, a souvenir accumulates the memories of everyone who's handled it—not just those of the final owner. Hundreds of people may have touched the same object before it came home stuffed in someone's luggage. Their energy has also been imprinted upon the memento; you may be bringing home more than a festive sombrero, my friend.

A handy kitchen knife may spring your psy-chometric skills into action; a blade trading hands reflects the joy—and possible sorrow—of days past. Since the kitchen is often the heart of the home, strong emotions are tied to its implements. Held daily, glasses, forks, and even potato peelers may be left with the memories of their former owner. If your cabinets are rumbling one night, you may want to tidy up before bed—someone's watching.

Flea markets and antique fairs: Rows of tables filled with old books, toys, and questionable beauty products may yield a bonanza for the paranormal collector. Items are often traded between vendors, and one small object may visit a large territory before it finds a home. If you see a table with little traffic, chat up the owner and see how their luck has been. Without realizing it, they may have been packing away a little unhappy stowaway ghost, resulting in poor sales.

Antique fairs are an excellent way for old books to travel. Highly marketable, they are traded and sold often enough that there may be a bit of paranormal residue hiding among the pages. Fairs frequently have higher-end furniture that may have a history attached as well. If you're looking to add to your collection and find a piece that feels right, discuss its history with the vendor to see if they have clues about where it came from. After purchasing the piece and getting it home, start your research. You may find that wingback has more drama attached beyond being just a lovely chair.

Walking sticks or canes are often found in markets and antique stores, making them an unusual way for a ghost to get around. Usually in constant use, and thus bonding with the item with the user, they were often decorated to reflect the owner's personality. Look for carvings, embellishments, or bands of metal that attach the handle to the shaft. (Metal is thought to attract and retain ghosts.) Discarded after the death of the owner, these items may be looking for a new home to haunt.

Thrift stores: Saving a bit of money digging through the racks of your favorite thrift store may be more than just bargain hunting. Being worn on the skin, clothing holds a residue that may not come off in the wash. Energy that is charged with emotion rubs off and is left for the next wearer. Hats and shoes especially seem to retain the memory of their former owners.

Is a favorite song grooved deeper into the black ridges an incantation to release the past? It's difficult to get a download of *I'm So Tired* to play "Paul is dead" backwards, so it's time to go old school and find a slightly warped disc and try your hand at scratching out a tune from the Devil. Vinyl records played over and over may gain an imprint of the owner. If your turntable is still groovy, get those record albums spinning and see if Earth, Wind & Fire can make your basement a boogie wonderland with a spiritual partner.

Antique shops: Don't let that Victorian horsehair love seat fool you; antique shops can be a hotbed of haunts. Memories shuffled from one generation to the next cling to the items they most loved—and won't part from. A box of photographs filled with images of the forgotten can stir up emotions. Tenderness, jealousy, joy—feelings don't die because the body has wasted away. Ghosts have been known to attach themselves to their former likeness, so make sure you're complimentary of those crazy hairstyles. Photographs containing orbs or undefined objects may also trap a bit of spiritual residue. If you're lucky, you may get one saying "cheese."

The instant-ancestors you purchased from an antique shop may have a little backstory. Paintings have been known to object when removed from homes they loved or even moved from a favorite room, such as the story of Aunt Pratt in *Haunted Housekeeping*. If buying a portrait, try to discover who the subject was and their story. If you find the frame on the floor the following morning, you may have brought home a grumpy grandfather.

Jewelry retains some of the most potent vibrations found with haunted objects. Metals, especially gold, are thought to be conductors of psychic energy. As the jewelry lays against the skin, it may absorb that energy and hold onto it.

Auctions: Some owners of haunted objects want to get rid of the goods fast. An auction, either online or local, can move an item out of the basement and into your hands in no time. Local auctions may not have the label "haunted" attached to a particular item, so take the time to visit the objects beforehand to try to get a feel for what's being offered. If you're interested in bringing home a haunted object, ask the auctioneer to keep an eye out for you. You could be first on their list for something special, and if the mojo is right, you may be able to bring home a new piece for your collection at a great price.

Online auctions are filled with promises of items ready to haunt the heck out of your house. Often accompanied by stories of mysterious events, random fires, and feelings of doom, the object is most likely something they found at the back of the sock drawer and want to make a little cash on. Multiple keywords in the title such as "witch-gypsy-ancient-spells-haunted-possessed" next to a fuzzy or dark photograph of the item can be a warning that while not being exactly haunted, it'll do a great job of becoming dust bait.

When determining if an online auction item is possibly haunted, keep this in mind: haunted objects are very rare and can be sold for large amounts of money to a buyer interested in occult or paranormal objects. If a seller claims to hold a trove of possessed items in their garage, how likely is it that they'd sell it for so little and have so many? Before purchasing the item, ask the seller for proof, other than just a weird feeling, that something is happening before you find yourself with a lighter wallet and a creepy doll. There are reputable sellers of haunted items online, of course, and they may be willing to work with you. By taking time to research the item and ask questions before buying, you and the seller may well become partners in the search for the truth behind that doll's painted smile.

Inheritance: Pieces passed down through the family may have special significance or have just been shuffled around so much that no one can remember why they held on to it in the first place. Part *Hoarders* episode and part sentimental journey, these objects are harder to part with if you have a relative attached. You may have won the lottery with that antique rocking chair, but your great-grandmother still has dibs on it.

Roadside finds: Old sofa left on a corner for the junk-man or possible paranormal treasure? Some items unceremoniously left for collection by the city may have a secret. That dollhouse left in a field could be there for a reason: the dolls are keeping the family up at night with their chatter. As you hone your instincts to recognize the potential for phantom activity in an object, don't be quick to pass over items dumped and left for dead. Many haunted things are abandoned because they come to people who aren't ready to appreciate their *unique* qualities. Please use common sense in bringing home any roadside find, as there may be something else living in that recliner that is more parasitical than paranormal.

SIGNS OF A HAUNTING

How can you tell if your house has a visitor who's not doing their share of the chores? Haunted objects often slide in unannounced and kick up their spectral heels in an otherwise peaceful home. Some of the signs of a haunting are subtle, while others yank the sheets off your bed and ask for a cup of tea. Have you experienced any of these signs after bringing home something new?

Sounds

Footsteps: Often associated with a residual haunting if they repeat a pattern over a few days to years, footsteps may also indicate that you have a wandering spirit on your hands (or a toddler looking for a late-night snack). Keep track of where the footsteps begin and end. Do they lead to the newest object in the house?

Doors opening and shutting on their own: A ghost may like to wander about its new surroundings, so don't be surprised if it gets a little curious and checks out what's behind closed doors. Hearing a door swing shut is more common than seeing any paranormal action, so keep your ears open on those quiet nights for phantom peepers.

Whispers or crying: An object may be a remembrance of a special day for a spirit. It's not uncommon to hear of haunted items becoming more active on an anniversary of significant dates of the former owner, so if you have knowledge of its history, spend a little extra time watching for signs of activity. Try capturing the sounds using a digital recorder, which can play back electronic voice phenomena (EVP) that may help you discover more about the ghost's past. You'll learn more about EVPs and how to record them in the investigation section.

Unidentified noises: It may be the house settling or the classic tree branch scraping against your window, but if you're experiencing noises such as thumping, knocking, or rapping on the walls that can't be attributed to bad water pipes or a raccoon making a summer home in your attic insulation, you may have a haunting. Don't jump to paranormal conclusions until you're sure you've crossed off all of the possible unexciting causes first. In older houses especially, rodents in the walls or poorly hung windows can be a source for phantom scratches, cold breezes, or whistles.

Smells

Food: Since food plays a huge role in many cultures, including family meals, wedding feasts, and wakes, kitchen implements brought into the home from another owner may stir up memories while you're stirring something on the stove.

Cigars, cigarettes, or pipes: The heavy scent of tobacco can stain the air with its haunting properties. Items such as a pipe are intimately connected with its owner, and when it is passed down through generations as an heirloom, memories may get fired up once more. The unmistakable aroma of a cigar can indicate a phantom visitor.

Gunpowder: Antique firearms may have the residue of old battles clinging to the barrel. Death may not part soldiers or hunters from their weapons just because they no longer have an itchy trigger finger. When bringing a gun into your home, its history may not be holstered so easily. Battlefield relics may also contain memories of the conflict: bullets, belt buckles, or personal belongings of the soldiers may have the deep emotional mark of what occurred during the fighting, such as pain, fear, or courage. The remnants of such may imprint the ghost and its final feelings upon the object.

Visions

First you see them—then you don't. Many times we'll catch what we may believe is a ghost out the corner of our eye only to shrug it off and blame the dog. Paranormal investigators believe that the act of materializing takes a lot of energy, so these short bursts of light or shadow may be the only way we can identify when a ghost is trying to get our attention. If you see a pattern emerging of when and where this phenomena occurs, jot it down and try to see if there's an association with an object you may have brought into your home. It may be linked to a special date or time of death of the owner.

Apparitions: If you are lucky enough to see a floating head or a full-length ghostly figure, note what it's wearing so you can follow up later with research. Apparitions come in various states of translucency, with some being no more than a wisp of smoke and others being so lifelike it could be difficult to tell that they don't have a pulse.

Missing items: Items vanishing only to appear days or weeks later at another location in the house is a common sign of a haunting. Different than a possessed possession, these objects may have just caught the fancy of a ghost who borrowed it for a bit. Toys, television remotes, and my children's homework have all been subjected to being caught in the loop, though I have my suspicions about the math worksheets. Other items such as coins and jewelry have appeared seemingly from nowhere to be found tucked away in a new location.

Electrical appliances: The blender may be trying to tell you something. Ghosts are thought to feed off of electromagnetic fields, thereby making it easy for them to manipulate and interrupt the flow from the source to the appliance. Much less complicated than gathering their energy to become an apparition, there are many reports of electronics reacting to what we believe are power-hungry ghosts. Faulty wiring may also be a factor, so please check with an electrician or change a bulb before deciding it's a sign from the beyond.

TYPES OF GHOSTS

The spirit world is classified into bite-sized bits to help us understand which ghost we're dealing with, some of which are: residual, intelligent, poltergeist activity, and shadow figures. To get a better look at what you may be harboring if you bring home your own piece of haunted history, let's break it down.

Residual: You've fallen into a time loop and can't get out. Most paranormal accounts of hauntings fall into the realm of the residual. A cacophony of footsteps, knocking on the walls, music playing by unseen hands, and even smells repeat themselves when the time—and audience—is right. There is no actual ghost interacting during a residual haunting—you've simply stepped into a memory and gotten a bit on your shoe.

Some objects seem to react to certain dates, such as anniversaries or a time of death, and we think that whatever is making it reach out and say "howdy" is trapped within its own vortex. The memory of an event or an emotion was so strong that it transferred to the item. That remembrance triggers a paranormal reaction that some of the living are attuned to and pick up on.

Intelligent: Now this is when a haunted item gets really interesting. Whispers, cold spots, even full-bodied apparitions revealing themselves could be signs that the afterworld is trying to get your attention. Attaching themselves to an object that meant something in their former lives can mean unfinished business needs to be attended to, and they're looking for someone sensitive enough to respond. If you search out haunted items, be aware that you may be taking on decades of drama wrapped up in an antique bow.

Intelligent hauntings are the stuff films are made of, but for good reason. Movies about ghosts have a giant chunk of the budget tied up in special effects, so while you may be excited to bring home an object that you suspect is haunted, you may get a fizzle instead of a bang.

Poltergeist: Aside from being a movie about creepy short people and bad television reception, the *poltergeist* (German for "noisy ghost") is the toddler of the spirit world. Often confused with an intelligent haunting, this type of ghost wreaks havoc by tossing items, slamming doors, or displaying phenomena such as raining rocks or toads upon the unlucky house. Usually centered on an adolescent child, a poltergeist is thought to be a subconscious tantrum of the subject. As the child grows older, the phenomenon subsides.

Shadow People: That flit of darkness seen out of the corner of your eye may be what's known as a shadow person. Usually described as a tall, humanoid gray-black shape with indistinct edges, they often appear to people in times of stress. Lurking alongside the living, shadow people have been reported as both ignoring those they unknowingly terrorize as they go about their business and possibly feeding off their energy. Both things sound rather unpleasant. It is thought that many of the paranormal reports of seeing ghosts stem from spying shadow people. They are not associated with a particular place or object and may, in fact, be random.

QUICK AND DIRTY INVESTIGATION TIPS

If you're experiencing any of the signs in the prior sections, it may be time to whip out the notebook and start your own investigation. And if you believe that the paranormal activity is centered on your newest knick-knack, settle in and get comfy.

Equipment: Breaking ghost hunting down to its basic tools, an investigator really only needs a few things: a notebook, pencil, watch, flashlight, camera or video equipment, voice recorder, compass, and snacks. Other tools such as EMF (electromagnetic field) detectors are great to have but can be expensive for ghost hunters just starting out.

Research: Every investigation begins with discovering more about the object (or area). Interviewing the former owner or their family is a good step in learning about what could possibly be attached. If you bought the item through the Internet, ask the seller if they are aware of any history of a haunting associated to the item. In some instances, the story surrounding the object makes the piece more valuable; other times the seller is afraid to share its quirky background for fear of never getting it off the shelf. If you've purposefully bought an object that is listed as "haunted," ask for the backstory; it could give you a heads-up before you see the actual floating head.

Starting Your Investigation

Many investigations are held at night not because it's spookier but because the day's noise is diminished and you're more likely to be able to focus on the task at hand. I prefer to conduct investigations with the lights on: how are you going to be able to see something move if you're stumbling around in the dark? There's no glory in a bruised shin, my friend.

To begin, choose a time when the house falls silent. It's always best to have at least one other person in the room with you—if they don't serve as ghost bait, then they will be able to verify what you've seen. After hours of staring at a haunted ceramic cupcake, your eyes can deceive you. Turn off all heating or air conditioning units so their sound won't interfere with your EVP (electronic voice phenomena) readings and check for drafts around windows. If you believe the object is prone to wandering, draw a chalk circle around its base so you will be able to tell if it has an urge to wiggle.

In your notebook, write down the time, date, whom you're with, and weather conditions. Storms are often associated with increased paranormal activity, so pay extra attention to your object at that time. You may find it's reaching out to say "hello" more often. It's tempting to chat with your partner during the wait, but this may cause you to miss something small associated with your haunted object. Have a set break time to compare notes and get a snack: there's nothing worse during an EVP session than a rumbling stomach mistaken as an otherworldly being when you play it back. Now is the time to start listening for odd noises: rapping, footsteps, and the like. Start keeping track of any changes that you experience during the session, such as the aforementioned noises, smells, or even feelings such as depression. When a spirit expels energy to make itself known to the living, it can be subtle, so pay attention in case there's no repeat performance. At the end of the predetermined time, compare notes with your partner as they may have noticed things that slipped by you.

Who Stole My Golden Aaaaaarm?

Electronic voice phenomena is a great way for investigators to make contact. Here's where the compass from your ghost hunting kit comes in: plan your questions in advance and place the compass on a flat surface near your object but away from electrical outlets or things that take a great amount of energy, such as televisions. Set the compass to true north and start your EVP session by stating your name, the date, the time, the room you're in, and whom you're with into your digital voice recorder. Begin asking questions into the microphone and watch the needle on the compass. If it wiggles, you may have a visitor. Noises from the living happen: a car driving by or a sneeze from a fellow investigator doesn't have to ruin the recording. When it happens, make sure to note it while the machine is recording so there are no false positives for activity.

What questions do you ask? It's like a first date: you want to be clever but not so clever that they think you're weird and make excuses to use the spectral bathroom and climb out of the window. You can begin by asking their name and age. Ask them to describe themselves—you may be able to tell what time period they're from by what they are wearing. Since your investigation is focused on an object, ask why this particular item is important. Leave a few seconds of silence between your questions so you'll be able to hear them on the recorder if they're able to answer. After a few minutes of questions, play back the recording and see if you have someone giving you a phantasmal high five.

Photographs: The Gotcha Moment

There's nothing like an orb to get the blood pumping during an investigation—unless the orb is really a blob of dust or a mold spore. Photographs during investigations are an important piece of the paranormal puzzle, but try to reduce the number of false images before you begin. Make sure reflective surfaces such as mirrors, television sets, jewelry, and bald heads are covered up so camera flashes don't bounce back as streaks of light. Wear dark-colored clothing because lighter colors may show up as a reflection of a ghostly figure. Watch those fingers: some spirits can look suspiciously like a thumb.

If you believe that activity is happening, point and shoot your camera where the action is. Take several photographs in sequence. If there's a glare from a mirror or passing car headlight, seeing if the light is still there in many of the photos can help prove or discount your theory.

Wrapping Up Your Investigation

Sometimes it can take weeks (or longer) to get any feedback from your spectral visitor. Keep your log handy to write down anomalies that you experience and see if there's a pattern to watch for in the future. Keep an open mind, be curious, and have fun with your newest adventure.

LIVING LARGE AS A MEDIUM

Some individuals have little choice than to recognize their own abilities to interact with the spirit world. If their gift is strong, it may be difficult to get the ghosts to pipe down. Their abilities to pick up on paranormal vibrations help them work with ghosts to send messages to those they've left behind or wrap up some unfinished business. Are they drawn to haunted objects more than the rest of us, or are the objects just better with the mojo to sway their buying habits?

Morrighan Lynne from Austin, Texas, uses her gift as a clairvoyant (all seeing) and clairaudient (all hearing) medium to help clients connect with those who have passed over. Coming from a family with unique talents in the psychic world themselves, she learned to develop her abilities after becoming aware of them in childhood. Being able to tap into the experiences a ghost went through previously, either emotionally or physically in that she is able to feel what they felt at certain times such as illness, Lynne uses all of her senses to communicate with the other side and interpret the messages they send her. In this way, she is able to fulfill her goal of assisting spirits who aren't quite ready to cross over with a little encouragement and a gentle push.

When encountering an object, Lynne says that depending on the spirit attached to the piece, she may be able to see how they died. Other times, an object "lights up" her vision, describing it as a white sound wave coming from the object to get her attention. That's when she settles in to acknowledge the spirit and listen to the tale they're trying to tell her.

"My very favorite story was when I was vacationing in Seattle with a friend and we went to a really cool antique shop. We were walking around, browsing and having a fun time. Suddenly, I walked into what felt like a bubble of energy that differed from the rest of the store. It stopped me in my tracks because at first, I didn't know what to make of it. So I just focused and took in whatever information I could pick up. My eyes drew me to this funky little statue to my right. As I began to lean over to pick it up, my stomach started hurting. Not like I was nervous, but like I was deathly ill. Knowing how my clairsentience works, I knew that this wasn't my stomach but someone else's. So I held the statue and tuned in harder…it was a woman, she died from stomach cancer. I saw the last few days of her life, the sadness, the gratitude, and her regrets. Everything she felt in those last days. After I got what I felt she wanted me to have, I put the statue down and walked out of the bubble," Lynne said.

"Continuing my browsing, I found myself in another bubble. This time I felt I couldn't breathe. I get that sensation a lot when working in the paranormal field, so I just have to tune in to get what kind of asphyxiation it is. This particular moment was a strangling. Tuning in further, I saw that the young man had hung himself. He felt so horrible, so sad and overwhelmed. But he wanted me to acknowledge him one last time. I looked around and found his object, picked it up and honored him. The lack of breathing decreased and I felt better, meaning he felt better. Then I continued to walk around.

"I found myself in the back looking at the old trunks and luggage, which I love. As I was touching them, one in particular kind of 'shocked' me. I held the handle and saw the entire young adult life of a beautiful girl who lived in a small town and always dreamed of going to New York to be on Broadway. I saw her say goodbye to her parents and get on a silver bus heading that way. I watched as she nervously stroked the handle while traveling, thinking about what was to come, wondering if she had made a mistake. I also saw how she was on stage, as more of a backup dancer, and that she had gotten mixed up with a very mean man. He was an abusive alcoholic and he eventually killed her one night after binge drinking. I was so moved by this and felt so connected to her that I bought the piece of luggage and had it shipped home safely. I still have it…even found an old bobby pin in the trunk that I cherish."

When asked about on how to work with a possessed possession, Ms. Lynne recommends taking it case by case.

"If they feel/think the energy around an object is negative or they feel uneasy around it, I would call someone to cleanse it properly. Different professionals have different methods. I prefer white light, sage, salt, and healing conversation," she said. "In my own experience, the spirit just wants to be acknowledged, to be heard. Sometimes that's enough to have them leave."

Psychometry

One method mediums employ is the use of psychometry. The ability to use touch to read the history of an object is powerful—the waves of emotion, sounds, memories, and smells can help someone sensitive to the object's vibrations decide to take it home or walk away quickly. Certain objects are more apt to hold on to this informational residue, such as metals, with gold being the most conducive to readings.

Much like a residual, or a time-loop, haunting, psychometry uses the same principles: psychics are able to access a time loop but are not able to interact with an actual ghost. They may be able to learn more about its story, but they cannot change an outcome nor talk a ghost out of haunting your china cabinet. One theory is that psychometry gives the psychic an ability to read an item's aura. No matter how solid an object appears, there are gaps between the molecules. Energy slips through those spaces and is interpreted by those sensitive enough to catch a shift in the vibrational force. If enough energy is expended toward an object, you may have gotten a little more bang for your inherited buck.

Jewelry worn close to the skin—such as rings, necklaces, and even eyeglasses—is especially helpful to the medium, as it is in contact with the original owner for long periods of time. My own experience with psychometry came during a meeting with a medium at a psychic fair. I was beginning my research into the paranormal and had no knowledge of touch readings. After I sat down, she asked for my eyeglasses as I wore no jewelry. Immediately, she told me I was going to marry a man named Bryan. Though the name was very familiar, I had no intention of marrying anyone anytime soon, much less to my younger brother, Bryan. I thanked her and continued my research, then promptly met and married a man named Bryan a few years later. I'm sure she was expecting a wedding invitation.

Developing the Gift of Psychometry

All talents take practice. Training yourself to receive impressions from an object you may believe is haunted is no different than playing the cello or perfecting haiku—except that the cello doesn't play itself. In order to gain the most accurate information, choose an item that is known to have only one owner. Place the item in your nondominant hand (if you are right-handed, put it in the left hand) and concentrate. Have a friend record what you relate. Visions, smells, and sounds may come across as a jumble, but tell them what you've experienced. What may be a small detail to you may be significant to someone else.

TWO

DEMONIC DOLLS AND CREEPY COLLECTIBLES

There's a mystery surrounding dolls that we can't shake since many adults now perceive them as the figurative fuel for nightmares. Whether we dressed them up, dragged them along to play dates as a child, or stuck them in a closet (wishing for them to just go away), these dolls left an indelible impression on our lives.

One reason people are generally attracted to and repelled by dolls, especially haunted dolls, is what they symbolize. When a doll is haunted, it usually involves a death of a child. Since most people are naturally drawn to protect and care for children, an early death of a boy or girl makes the story more tragic. What's left behind are the toys that were once held in her hands or stood watch on a bedside nightstand, only to be discarded and forgotten after the child is laid to rest. However, some toys may not be forgotten by their original owners, who have decided to move on with their playthings.

A collection of dolls. Perhaps one of them is haunted? Courtesy of the Library of Congress.

Aside from the basic fear many adults have of tiny maniacal mummers, toys are often on the list of haunted items. Is it because we assign innocence to the objects, making it even more alarming when they suddenly interact after years of being abandoned on a shelf? What can turn a once-beloved toy into something to fear? Take one last look around your child's bedroom. I think that stuffed bear was giving you the stink-eye.

A WHISPER IN MY SOUL

For Beth, a writer from Eureka Springs, Arkansas, her experience with a haunted toy was comforting. After purchasing a small plastic Scooby-Doo candy topper with a light-up heart to add to her collection of Scooby-Doo memorabilia twelve years ago, she received confirmation that love is never far away.

"The year the event happened, I was very emotionally attached to my Scooby-Doo collection, and the candy topper was on my display shelf behind my desk. The week before the anniversary of my father's passing, a friend and I were discussing him. My friend asked if, after more than twenty years, I still felt the loss. I responded with a flippant 'no,' then that night I cried and told my father out loud that I still missed him," she said

"A couple of days before the anniversary, I noticed the candy topper heart was lit up. I checked it and turned it off, thinking the switch must have hit the shelf and turned on. The next day I went into my home office, and the topper was on again. I brought the collectible out to my husband in the next room, who examined it, took out the batteries, and looked at the metallic contacts. He said it looked fine, and without the batteries, it would stop turning on. I put it back on the shelf.

"That night I went into the office to get something, and it was on. I was a little freaked, so I asked my husband to come look at it. He came back to my office and confirmed that there were no batteries in it, but the heart was still glowing. I placed it back on the shelf. The heart stayed lit all through the next day, which was the anniversary, and I felt a comforting presence in the room with me. I believe it was my father checking in with me and letting me know everything was all right. The glow stopped that night."

Though Beth has experienced other phenomena in the house, such as hearing her name called, she never witnessed the heart lighting up again and believes the heart was a chosen to reach out to her at a time when she needed comforting most. Since then, she has noticed paranormal activity in the week surrounding the anniversary of her father's death.

It's not the first time her father has made his presence known to his family. In the year following his passing, Beth reported that his photograph would fly off the back of a shelf in the family living room. She felt her mother sensed that he wanted them to move on with their lives—after packing away the photograph, the phenomena ceased.

Experiencing even more paranormal activity after the death of her brother in 2002, Beth acknowledges that she could be a bit sensitive to the otherworld, saying, "I've had many moments in my life when I felt something before it happened, like a whisper in my soul."

THE ENCHANTED DOLL FOREST

For business owner Suzanne Kraus Mancuso of the Enchanted Doll Forest in upstate New York, her brush with the paranormal came with a price. Opening her doll shop in March 2012, she joined other antique vendors in sharing the converted nineteenth-century dairy farm's outbuilding. Immediately after settling into the space, Mancuso noticed little things: "At first it was a simple as something being 'moved' or missing—then it progressed to hearing my name being called, lights burning out, and the radio would go off and on many times throughout the day. But what really made me contact the paranormal team was when my co-worker stood up to go out to her car—as soon as she crossed the threshold, the radio went on. As soon as she crossed the doorway to come back inside, the radio went off. My mouth dropped open and I was shocked—but I knew I wasn't alone there."

Her doll business was fueled by a steady influx of dolls acquired by tag sales, eBay, and other auctions, though some dolls were simply dropped off. She believes it was the combination of these dolls together in the shop that really stirred things up. Keeping a diary of suspected paranormal activity, Mancuso saw a pattern forming: some mornings she'd come in and find certain dolls scattered on the ground or in piles in exactly the same spot in the center of the store, and twice she found dolls missing their heads. While working, she often felt like she was being watched and was also haunted by the sound of breaking glass and disembodied laughter behind her.

Mancuso couldn't explain any of that activity. But in May 2012, she described an event—one that clearly indicated someone wanted to get her attention.

"I was cleaning the floor today [by] vac—found a dead mouse on floor—took outside [and] threw [it] over the fence. Ten minutes later I found the SAME dead mouse in the same spot—threw it over the fence. Ten minutes later I found the pine cone—same spot," she said.

By the summer of 2012, Mancuso had had enough of wandering dolls and music boxes that played a tune without the help of a winding hand. A small bear wearing a blue T-shirt had been the repeated victim of being tossed around the shop, so in July she threw it away along with the music box, hoping the haunting would stop, but by then she knew she needed help. She contacted two local paranormal teams to investigate and the activity seemed to increase after they'd left—voodoo dolls were found on the floor after being "ripped off [the] wall" and the doll piles were becoming more frequent. Keeping a diary of the paranormal activity, she listed two newly acquired dolls as crying by themselves while others flew across the shop as she watched.

Mancuso has since moved the Enchanted Doll Forest to a new location. The dolls are still active, though not to the same degree.

As a seller, Mancuso's business relied on being upfront with her customers. Dolls that showed the most activity were described as haunted, giving a heads-up to customers who brought the doll home that they could be in for a bumpy ride. She has found that collectors of haunted items are eager to learn more about her experiences and will pay anything to have a possessed doll in their homes. As for her business, however, Mancuso is done with the realm of haunted dolls. Downsized but still selling, she feels the activity has ruined her business. "I don't recommend haunted things to anyone—and be prepared to deal with THINGS afterwards," she said.

ANNABELLE

Passing an antique store in 1970, Donna's mother couldn't resist buying the large rag doll with round button eyes as a birthday gift for her college-aged daughter. Donna loved the doll and displayed it prominently in her bedroom of the apartment she shared with a fellow nursing student, Angie. Days later, the women noticed something peculiar about the doll. After making her bed each morning, Donna would place the doll—legs straight out and arms to the sides—on her bed, but when she returned in the evening, the legs and arms would be positioned differently. The limbs would be crossed or the doll's arms would be folded in its lap.

A week or so passed, and each day the doll would change its position. Donna tested the doll by purposefully placing the limbs in crossed positions to see if they'd be in a similar state when she returned. Not only did she find the arms and legs uncrossed, the doll would be found hunched over or knocked to one side.

Eventually, the girls found the doll making a break for it in the front room. Returning home one night, Donna and Angie discovered the doll sitting in a chair near the front door—kneeling. Other times, they would find it sitting on the sofa.

The doll started to leave notes around the apartment. Written in pencil on parchment paper, of which they had neither in the house, they found messages pleading for help. "HELP US" and "HELP LOU" were scrawled in childlike handwriting across the yellowed paper.

Thinking the doll's antics were a trick being played on them by someone with access to their apartment, Donna and Angie began to mark positions on the doors and windows to track anyone coming into the room. Never finding evidence of a person entering the apartment, they began to get scared.

One night, the women found blood on the back of the doll's soft cloth hand—and three drops of blood on its chest. They decided to contact a medium to see if she could explain the odd occurrences surrounding the doll. The psychic told them a young girl had died on the property. The girl's name was Annabelle Higgins, a seven-year-old. Annabelle had decided she'd liked the rag doll and felt the students were able to relate to her, the psychic continued, so she had possessed the doll to be near them. The women called the doll Annabelle from that moment on and treated the expressionless toy as if it were a child. They felt it was no longer a plaything—it was a child in need of love.

Lou, a friend of Angie and Donna's, had never felt comfortable around the doll. While he couldn't determine why he'd rather be in a separate room from Annabelle, he should have listened to his instincts. Napping on the couch in their front room one day, Lou dreamed of the doll. Feeling himself wake up, he looked around the room and then saw Annabelle at his feet. The doll began to climb up his legs, moving over his chest until it reached his neck. In his dream, he saw the soft arms touch either side of his throat and the horror of himself being strangled by the rag doll. Waking in terror, he knew the doll had to go.

Later, while preparing for a trip the next day, Lou was alone in the apartment with Angie. Hearing noises coming from Donna's bedroom, Lou suspected they'd finally catch whatever had been playing with the doll and discover who was behind the tricks. Quietly opening the door to the room, Lou saw nothing out of place, except that instead of being in her normal place on top of the bed, Annabelle was lying crumpled in a corner. As he walked further into the room and closer to the doll, he felt a dark presence behind him. Spinning around to face the attacker, Lou fell to the ground as Angie ran in to find her friend bleeding. Peeling away the material of his shirt, they found seven claw-like marks on his chest, the scratches burning like fire into his flesh. Remarkably, the wounds healed completely within a day or two, but they knew they needed help to deal with whatever had possessed the doll.

Donna contacted the local Episcopal Church, which suggested they contact Ed and Lorraine Warren, the founders of the New England Society for Psychic Research. Ed, a demonologist, and Lorraine, a trance medium, were intrigued by the case. After discussing Annabelle's history with Donna and Angie, the Warrens determined that the doll was demonically possessed and this was not a simple haunting. They felt that whatever had taken control of the doll had done so by emotionally manipulating the girls by telling them, via the medium, that it was the spirit of a child locked inside, thus giving the demon a way to enter the apartment. Feeling that Donna and Angie were in danger, the Warrens offered to take the doll away from the house.

On the way home, the Warrens had a tussle with their back-seat driver. The car stalled or swerved on curves, making the journey dangerous. Finally, Ed Warren removed a vial of holy water from his bag and sprinkled it liberally over the possessed doll in the back seat. The rest of the drive home was uneventful. At their home, Annabelle sat in a chair next to Ed's desk, though he reported that it would often move to different rooms, even levitating when it first arrived.

A special case was built for the doll, and it moved to the Warren's Occult Museum, where she has remained quiet ever since. Or has she? The doll may be to blame for the death of a museum visitor. Hearing the story of Lou's experiences with Annabelle, a young man taunted the doll by asking it to scratch him and banging on its case. Escorted from the museum with a warning to respect what he didn't understand, the visitor and his girlfriend left on his motorcycle for home. Not long after leaving the Occult Museum, the young man was the victim of an accident as his motorcycle ran off the road and hit a tree, killing him instantly.

THE BROKEN-FACED DOLL: MANDY

Museums are spooky places. There's history attached to every object and a story that most of us will never hear. Curators don't like to talk about some artifacts in their collections in terms of "haunted" or "possessed," but strange things often happen at night when the doors are tight and items are once again left to their memories. Locked away in their cases, are some objects there for their protection—or ours?

Mereanda, or Mandy, as she's better known, came to the Quesnel & District Museum and Archives in British Columbia in 1991. Donated by a woman who thought the museum would be better able to care for the 1920s-era porcelain doll, Mandy was brought to former curator, Ruth Stubbs. In a *Quesnel Advocate* article, Stubbs recalled that the donor told her that Mandy had belonged to her grandmother but didn't want her own daughter to play with it since it had started to fall apart. And there was something else—since the doll had come to the donor, odd things had been happening at her home. Windows would be found open when closed shut moments before, and in the basement, she would hear a baby cry only to find the wind blowing through another open window and no child to comfort. Stubb's unease at accepting the toy was only an inkling of what was to come.

The doll's soft body was torn and its dress filthy, but the staff at the museum were used to receiving items needing repair or cleaning. What bothered them was Mandy's face. Large cracks scarred its features, running from her temple to across the eye and cheeks; it looked more like a battered child than a doll that had been cherished. Once beautiful, Mandy was not showing her age well with flaking paint and slightly bulging eyes, giving her an ominous look. Photographs were routinely snapped, with the doll's picture being taken at a variety of angles and positions. The photographer and her boyfriend reportedly felt uneasy while Mandy was in the room but couldn't put a finger on just why. The next day, they walked into the photo lab to find pencils and pens scattered all over the floor, looking like, according to Ruth Stubbs, "a small child had had a temper tantrum." The photographer soon reported hearing a loud sigh behind her while in the lab and jumped as something fell off a shelf. Apparently Mandy didn't like having her photo taken.

Other staff had problems after Mandy arrived. Office supplies would go missing, and footsteps would echo in the building when they thought they were alone. Though not easily frightened, they kept a close eye on the baby doll to see what her next trick would be.

With no permanent display area ready for Mandy at the museum, the doll sat facing the entrance in a makeshift case. Patrons entering the building were greeted with her slightly off-putting face and reported feeling as if her eyes followed them around the room or experiencing feelings of sadness. Some visitors claimed her head and fingers would move on their own, her aged eyes blinking as the patrons moved away from the doll with the broken face. Later, she was moved to another part of the museum but not with other dolls, as it was whispered among the staff members that she might harm them. Mandy has been blamed for a rash of missing artifacts, and a few lunches, that somehow showed up elsewhere in the museum.

Ruth Stubbs decided to contact the donor who had dropped off the little troublemaker. She learned that after the dump and drive, the woman never heard the baby in the basement again nor found a stray breeze in her house due to Mandy needing fresh air. Now a celebrity, Mandy has been featured on television shows that watch for a wave or a spinning head. The museum welcomes visitors to make their own decisions regarding a doll that may have seen too much and tells its secrets to no one.

ROBERT, THE HAUNTED DOLL OF KEY WEST

Locked within a glass cage of crazy at the Fort East Martello Museum is a century-old resident of Key West,

Florida, with a chip on his shoulder. Robert's story began around the turn of the twentieth century as a gift to a young boy from a servant working in his home. Standing at just over four feet tall, the doll was handmade to resemble his namesake, a child named Robert Eugene (Gene) Otto, with a soft, painted face and wearing a jaunty sailor suit. But was Robert a simple gift or was Gene a pawn in a game of revenge and voodoo?

The Ottos were a wealthy family, building the home in 1898 that would come to be known as the Artist House. While they enjoyed a privileged lifestyle on the small island, Mr. and Mrs. Otto were rumored to have treated the help very poorly. A servant girl, reported to have come from an island rich in voodoo tradition, made the doll for the young boy with a purpose: to create a friend for Gene that would drive him mad and, perhaps, hurt the child as a parting gift to Mrs. Otto for the cruelty the servant had endured.

Gene and Robert were inseparable. Giving the doll his first name, Gene played endlessly with Robert, replacing other children in his life with a grinning facsimile of a real boy. Often seen accompanying the family on outings or sitting at the table next to Gene at mealtimes, Robert quickly became more than just a simple plaything.

Soon, the servants whispered between themselves that Gene could be heard talking to Robert while alone in his room. The door shut, they strained to hear the quiet words of the boy through the wood, only to hear a voice respond that was completely unlike the child's. Alarmed, they watched and waited for what would come next.

Unexplained events began to happen at the house. Items would go missing and unused bedrooms would be found torn apart, their bedding thrown around the room. Gene's other toys suffered as well—the household would hear laughter late at night only to find his toys damaged and disfigured the next morning. But each time Gene was to be punished, he would blame the doll. With their son insisting that the doll did it, his parents began to feel uneasy around Robert's painted smile. They began to wonder if the giggles they heard around the house didn't belong to their son but to his wool-stuffed playmate.

Those close to the family were worried. Gene's attachment to the doll wasn't normal and the destruction that followed in the wake of the large toy had to be stopped. Convinced that Robert's influence upon their young son was unhealthy, the family banished Robert to the attic, packed away in a large box. Soon afterward, an aunt died of a stroke, and while no one really believed that the doll had a hand in her death, no one was taking any chances—Robert returned to Gene's side once more.

Gene's parents passed away, and he continued to live in Artist House with his childhood companion. The town knew of his attachment to the doll, some wondering if

Robert hadn't allowed Gene to fully grow up. Schoolchildren hurried by the large house on the corner of Eaton Street, frightened to see if Robert's glassy eyes were trained on them from the turret window as they passed by on their way home.

Eventually, Gene married and became a well-known artist in the Key West community. His wife Anne, however, wasn't ready to share her life with a creepy doll. When she insisted that Robert be placed back in the attic, Gene complied with his wife's wishes, but he knew the doll would never give up his best friend so easily. Late at night, the couple would hear footsteps running across the attic floor and the sound of a child's wild laughter ring throughout the house. Friends of the Ottos stopped coming by, frightened of what they may hear or see scurrying past them up the stairs and heading to the attic. As the couple grew older, Robert's grip on the household was tightening. Gene was rumored to have spent most of his day in his childhood room in the turret, playing with Robert and keeping the doll's evil nature at bay.

After Gene Otto's death in 1974, his wife rented out Artist House with the condition that the doll remain undisturbed in the attic. Stories swirled around the mysterious footsteps and laughter heard coming from the top room; the townsfolk were fascinated yet scared of what was happening at the grand house. Tenants never stayed long.

Not comfortable sharing space with a possessed doll, they often moved quickly as they realized it too could come for them. A plumber who had been working in the attic was reported as saying he had heard the doll laughing behind his back. When he spun around to confront the noise, he saw that Robert had moved across the room on his own. He claims he wasn't frightened but admitted that some of his tools were probably still up there. Good choice.

Even when the house sat empty, neighbors told of hearing "evil giggles" and watching as the doll ran from window to window in the turret room to stare at those who strolled past on the street. Later that year, the house was sold to Myrtle Reuter, who found the doll in a box and kept him with her as her own "best friend." Twenty years later, Ms. Reuter gave him away to the Fort East Martello Museum, sharing stories of how she believed Robert moved around the house under his own power. As Robert settled in to his new home, the notorious doll became a celebrity.

As he sits placed in a special case, letters from visitors cover the wall behind him to apologize for disbelieving in his powers and their subsequent bad luck. As he sits and seemingly waits for the next visitor, he unnerves those who make the trip to see the doll. Cameras malfunction and electronic devices go awry if permission isn't asked before photographing this strange toy. It is said, though, that if you ask nicely before shooting, he may tip his head to one side to give you consent to begin.

Various ghost hunting groups and media outlets have attempted to get to the bottom of the mystery surrounding Robert. Investigators from The Atlantic Paranormal Society (TAPS), during the filming of one of their shows, reported finding an aura of blue and purple surrounding the doll. Auras aren't found around inanimate objects, so how did Robert manage to emit enough energy to be picked up on film?

Employees at the museum have often heard Robert giggling behind them as they walk the otherwise silent hallways at closing time. On occasion, they'll hear tapping, only to find Robert's hand pressed against the glass of his box—but is it a friendly greeting or a warning? There are stories of his face turning from a gentle smile to one of irritation and a malevolent frown, facing down those who come to mock the doll face to face. When coming to Robert to get an answer to a question, some museum visitors have later reported having terrible dreams where Robert gives them what they want, but in the scariest way possible.

He's come up missing a few times, only to be found within his case later. He may be visiting the Artist House to check on how his former home—now a bed-and-breakfast—is doing. If he does, he may run into the spirit of Anne, who is rumored to guard the turret room since Robert's absence. Guests at the B&B have told the staff that they've felt a gentle presence in the bedroom watching over them as they slept or heard soft footsteps pacing the floor, perhaps keeping watch against Robert's imminent return.

While he is on permanent display at the Fort East Martello Museum year-round, the museum invites curious visitors to have a special viewing of their most famous artifact each October at the Custom House Museum, the headquarters of the Key West Art and Historical Society. During that month, he is said to be at his most active, so active in fact, that the museum staff has been known to leave a few peppermints in his case to keep him from misbehaving. They cannot explain why there may be a couple candies missing in the morning. Perhaps Robert has a sweet tooth?

THE ISLAND OF HAUNTED DOLLS

An island in the tangle of canals in Mexico's Xochimilco district, south of Mexico City, is where nightmares go to grab a margarita before heading back to work. Thousands of dolls, their limbs missing or replaced with another's arm or head, gently sway in the soft wind and welcome visitors with their dead eyes. The trees are filled with tiny bodies hanging in their mutilated glory, an offering to the small girl who drowned in the canals surrounding Teshuilo Lake in the 1920s.

Don Julian Santana Barrera, a man who had retreated to the deserted island in the late 1950s, had made the small spit of land his own to escape the pressure of family and society. There, he learned from those nearby of the dark legends of the girl who had succumbed to the water and died while playing with friends; her spirit continued to play along the banks of the canal, refusing to pass over. Alone on the island, Barrera began to hear the dead child's voice. The lonely girl asked him to find dolls for her to play with. Soon he began to scour the canals, plucking discarded and unloved dolls from the water as they floated by and picking through garbage dumps on rare trips to the mainland to keep her happy and him from madness.

For fifty years, Barrera brought dolls to the ghostly girl, believing that the voice that whispered to him was now protecting him from the spirits that were invading the dolls. Their heads twisting within their nooses or from posts he had impaled the soft bodies onto, the dolls were now torturing Barrera rather than appeasing the spirit of the child. As the forest claimed the dolls' bodies, they began to disintegrate in the harsh weather. Blisters from the sun pockmarked their plastic faces while mold clung to fabric dresses and rotted away whatever love had once been attached to the doll through a child's long-ago hug. Spiders invaded hollow heads, their nests filling up sockets of eyes that were plucked out by birds or lost in the currents of the canal. It was now their voices he heard more often than the drowned girl's. Voices called to him, wanting him to join them in the depths beneath the muddy swirls of the canal.

The island was forgotten to time. Barrera continued to build his home there with the dolls, even constructing a small hut to shield his more prized dolls from the elements to make the ghost girl happy and mollify the evil spirits. In 1990, the area was declared a national heritage site and water traffic resumed along the canals, passing the island. Eventually the island became known as *La Isla de las Muñecas* (The Island of Dolls). Passersby told of hearing voices as they floated by, believing they came from the dolls as they stared from their perches in the trees.

On April 21, 2001, Barrera and his nephew, Anastasio, were fishing on the island. Leaving to run errands, Anastasio returned later to find his uncle floating face down in the same canal where the child had drowned years before. It's now rumored that his spirit wanders the island, finally joining the girl he had catered to for so long.

The island is open for visitors to wander through the odd shrine. Anastasio welcomes anyone who makes the long trip and wants to hear the stories of how the dolls seemingly come alive after the heat of the day is extinguished, their voices carrying on the water—asking you to join them.

THREE

RESTLESS BONES

Nothing could be more intimately connected with people than their own bones. Haunted objects such as skulls keep the party going long after the body goes cold. Skeletal remains that wouldn't stay put in the grave sometimes have a way of showing up in the ancestral homes of England. Often, the last wish of the dying is tied to a location—to return to the house they love or to their faraway home. If moved, the skulls made their displeasure known by the triple threat of storms, poltergeist activity, and ear-splitting screams.

In some cases, the skull has turned into a gruesome good-luck charm for the family—along the same lines as the ravens of the Tower of London, whose legend states that as long as they are present on the grounds, the kingdom will never fall—the skull-keepers believe that they are safe from great harm if the skull stays safely within the walls of the home.

Skulls aren't the only bits making a fuss. The tumbling coffins of Barbados and the Baltic island of Saaremaa kept villagers on their toes. Each time they opened the crypts to place a new member within its walls, they were faced with seeing if the previously placed corpses were trying to rejoin the living and escape their stone tomb. How did suicide factor into the story of these crypts, and why can't science solve the mystery of these century-old phenomena?

Deep within the recesses of Paris' underground tunnels lie the catacombs of the city's dead. Now a popular tourist attraction, visitors claim to have experienced more than a brush with history. They may have had a spirit accompany them with a little extra *joie de vive*.

WARDLEY HALL

What was found in a wall of an ancient manor house in the eighteenth century has spooked generations of families living within the stone confines of Wardley Hall. As the wall crumbled, the box that housed a grisly skull fell to the floor and was examined. A servant, thinking it was an animal skull, threw it into the moat. That night, a storm raged over Wardley Hall and the owner of the great house believed the skull was screaming for it to be returned to its home within the safety of the walls. He may have heard of the manor house's curse of a screaming skull. Sensibly, he had the moat drained the next day, found the skull, and had it tucked away back into the comfort of the house.

The mystery of the skull starts with exactly whose shoulders it sat upon while they were alive. One legend tells of it belonging to the seventeenth-century royalist Roger Downes, whose family lived at Wardley Hall during the time of the English Civil War. A man of uneven temper, he vowed during a drunken spell in London to kill the first man he came upon. An unfortunate tailor was killed instantly as he came into view, skewered with Downes's sword as he walked by. Downes was arrested and tried for the murder but was set free due to his sway at court. He wasn't free for long; Downes again visited London soon afterward and chose to challenge the wrong man to a duel on Tower Bridge. The watchman of the Bridge severed the head from Downes's neck in one stroke and dumped the body into the dark water of the River Thames below. His head was then sent to Wardley Hall in a wooden box. This story was woven into legend but was later disproved in 1779 when his coffin was opened and Downes's head was still firmly attached.

So whose head was hiding behind the wall panels at Wardley Hall and making a commotion? It most likely belonged to Father Edward Ambrose Barlow, a Benedictine monk. Francis Downes (Roger's son) and his wife were devout Catholics at dire odds with the Roundheads (supporters of Parliament who were mostly Puritans and Presbyterians) during the Civil War. However, in secret, Downes allowed Barlow to perform Mass in their chapel. After eluding religious persecution for over two decades, Barlow was discovered at nearby Morleys Hall officiating Mass in 1671; he was hanged and quartered for his faith and his head removed. The head was put on display at either Manchester church or Lancaster Castle as a warning against going against those in power. It is believed that Francis Downes later removed the skull and returned with it to Wardley Hall to be hidden away in a small chamber cut into the walls to be eventually forgotten and Downes's religious leanings safe.

Is the skull still secure within the walls of the Hall? After stories of the head's fateful nights away from the Hall—including its burial, burning, or being smashed into pieces only to be discovered the next day on the grounds waiting to be let back in, we'll just have to wait for the next time someone gets itchy throwing fingers.

BETTISCOMBE SKULL

One of the louder haunted heads is the infamous Bettiscombe Skull housed near Lyme Regis in Dorset, England. The tale began in the late seventeenth century after the death of a servant who had been brought to England from the West Indies.

There were rumors of bad blood between the servant and the owner of Bettiscombe Manor, Azariah Pinney. Gossip hinted that the two men had fought, resulting in the injury of the servant. Begging from his deathbed to be returned to his homeland for burial, he threatened to curse the household if his final wishes were not carried out. Perhaps feeling a bit of remorse or simply not wanting to push his luck, Pinney agreed to the man's wishes. But after the servant's death and not wanting to incur the expense of shipping the body across the sea, Pinney had the servant buried in the local churchyard, not far from the house. Shortly afterward, the small town was subjected to anguished moans and screams coming from the graveyard. Identifying the sounds as coming from the fresh plot, the locals demanded that the manor take responsibility and move the corpse to its own property. Digging the body up, they transported it back to the grounds. After repeated attempts to re-bury the body on the manor grounds had met with the same high-pitched results, they placed it high in a barn loft to slowly rot. The skeleton fell to pieces, even as the skull remained intact. Before long, all that was left was the gruesome head of a very unhappy ghost.

The skull eventually found itself on a staircase leading to the manor's roof, despite multiple attempts to rid the house of the skull. One resident, tired of the cater-wauling, threw it into a nearby pond hoping it would sink to the bottom. That night, the manor's windows rocked with the skull's screams. The next morning, they drug the pond to find the offensive head and brought it back into the house, resigned to their fate. Other times when removing the skull, the paranormal activity that accompanied the screaming in the house became so prevalent that it was unbearable, prompting them to once again return the skull within the walls. Perhaps the most disturbing legend is of the time the skull was dropped into a deep hole dug on the property: the next morning, the skull had tunneled itself out and was found by the groundsmen, waiting to be brought inside.

Also associated with the Screaming Skull of Bettiscombe Manor is a phantom coach that leaves the house to rush along the road to the church where the body was once buried. The locals refer to this phenomenon as the "funeral procession of the skull."

Science always ruins a good story. In the 1960s, Professor Gilbert Causey of the Royal College of Surgeons examined the skull and believed it actually belonged to a woman in her early twenties from the nearby Iron Age settlement of Pilsdon Pen. Just as gruesome as the tale of the screaming skull, it is thought she may have been a victim sacrificed to bring prosperity to the region, as severed heads thrown down a well were sometimes offered as tribute to water spirits.

The skull is now regarded as a good-luck charm for the house. To keep it safe and cut down on sleepless nights, it's reportedly kept in a box and locked away in a drawer.

BURTON AGNES HALL

There was no place like home for Katherine (Anne) Griffith. Watching her father's magnificent manor house in Yorkshire, Burton Agnes Hall, being built from 1598 to 1620, the girl had grown up among each stone being placed and each room furnished to reflect the taste of the late Renaissance period of Elizabeth I of England. One of three sisters, Anne walked with them to visit friends, the St. Quintins, at Harpham about a mile away from the Hall. Near St. John's Well, they were attacked and robbed by cutthroats: Anne, refusing to part with her mother's ring, was viciously beaten. Carried back to Burton Agnes Hall, Anne wove in and out of delirium. Before dying five days later, she made her sisters promise to keep part of her with them forever, wanting to "remain in our beautiful home as long as it shall last." I'm sure they weren't expecting that part to be her grinning skull, but they vowed nonetheless to keep her peaceful and quiet, not realizing that "quiet" was a matter of interpretation.

After Anne's death, they decided to forgo the promise and bury her intact body in the local churchyard. Soon, odd noises erupted within the great hall, making life unbearable. Her ghost was said to wander Burton Agnes, screaming and moaning, pleading to come home. A few weeks later, Anne's body was disinterred. It was discovered that while her body had little decay since her death, the skull had been severed and was devoid of hair or skin. Returning with the skull to the manor house, they locked it away in a cupboard, where it remained, apparently satisfied and quietly happy.

Attempts to remove the skull occurred throughout the years. In one instance, a story tells of a maid, who didn't believe in such nonsense as a haunted head, wrapping the skull in rags and tossing it into a passing wagon full of cabbages. Immediately, the horses pulling the wagon came to a full stop and refused to move until the wagon was searched and the skull retrieved. Another time, it was buried in the garden, but her ghost, now known as "Owd Nance," resumed its miserable wailing until the skull was dug up and brought back into the house. After that, it was hidden within the panels of the walls. The trust at Burton Agnes Hall is hesitant to wake the dead by searching for the skull, believing it may be still within the great hall, and is content to think that the spirit of Anne is quiet at last.

THE CALGARTH SKULLS

The price of a view came with a plan for execution. The bucolic setting of the Cook cottage near Lake Windermere in Cumbria was the pride of the hardworking couple. Poor but happy, Kraster and Dorothy Cook lived within their means and were content to farm the land. Their neighbor, Myles Phillipson, was a wealthy landowner and magistrate. For years, he had tried to convince the Cooks to sell him their plot of land so he could build a grander house and extend his own farming ventures with their acreage. And for years they refused.

Their rejection turned Phillipson against them and a plan was hatched with his wife to gain possession of the Cooks' land. The magistrate visited the Cooks at their home a week before Christmas, telling them that he had decided to build his home elsewhere and that to mend their rift, he invited them to join his family for a Christmas Day celebration. The Cooks, while suspicious, decided to attend the party as a gesture of good will.

The party was magnificent. No expense was spared as the Phillipson's wealth was on display for their guests. Vast amounts of food, rich linens, and the family silver graced the table. Feeling out of place, the Cooks said little to the other partygoers, though it's told Kraster's eyes fell upon a silver cup throughout the evening. After dinner, the party moved on to dancing and games in the other rooms, though the Cooks stayed behind in the dining room, not eager to join the others in small talk. Deciding on a proper amount of time to pass so as not to offend their new friend, they returned home.

As the sun rose the next morning, soldiers arrived at the cottage with orders from Phillipson to arrest the couple for the theft of the silver cup. As they were dragged from their home, a soldier produced the vessel—most likely planted while they searched the home—as proof of their guilt. Kept apart for the next week, Kraster and Dorothy saw each other next in court where they heard the case against them.

Phillipson's wife was the prosecution's primary witness. She told the court how the Cooks had admired the cup and had discussed its beauty with Mr. Cook during dinner, and then their servants told how the couple had stayed behind while the others had moved out of the dining room to enjoy the party. The soldiers who had searched the house testified that the cup had been found on the property, sealing the fate of the Cooks. Theft was an offense punishable by death, but as magistrate, Myles Phillipson could have chosen to have them imprisoned and seize their land. Phillipson chose to silence the Cooks' protests forever on the gallows.

Before being dragged from the court, Dorothy Cook was recorded as saying, "Hark's to here, Myles Phillipson, that teenie lump o' land is t'dearest grund a Phillipson has ever bowte. For ye shall prosper niver maur, yersl, nor yan of o't breed. And while Calgarth's strong woes shall stand, we'll haunt it day and neet." Days later, she and her husband died on the gallows at Appleby.

The Phillipsons wasted little time in taking possession of the land, pulling down the wee cottage and building their new home, Calgarth Hall, in its place. A year had passed since the Cooks' death, the couple forgotten as snow blanketed their graves and fires warmed the new owners of their land. To celebrate the completion of the Hall, a Christmas banquet was planned. Guests crowded the rooms to join in the good fortune of their hosts. Leaving the party for a moment, Mrs. Phillipson ascended the staircase to her rooms to fetch a jewel. Rounding the corner, she discovered the grisly remains of two skulls. Ordering them to be thrown into the courtyard, she returned to the party thinking it was a joke played upon them by insensitive guests.

During the night, screaming throughout the house awakened the Phillipsons, though they could not find the source. As dawn approached, they saw the two skulls sitting on the stair steps and quickly threw them into a nearby pond. Again the screaming continued during the following night and again the skulls appeared on the staircase by morning. News of the curse spread throughout the village; their friends and business partners shunned the Phillipsons as they remembered Dorothy Cook's dying words. The once-prosperous family fell into ruin—Dorothy's revenge was taking hold of their lives. After Myles Phillipson's death, the skulls appeared only twice a year—Christmas and the anniversary of the Cooks' death. His heirs couldn't escape the tangled reach of the curse. Once, during a dinner party, the doors blew open to the dining room. Legend has it that two skulls rolled across the floor, frightening the guests and reminding their host that they will never be dismissed again.

Years passed and Calgarth Hall became neglected, and parts of the great house crumbled as the fortunes of the family could not keep up with the cost of repairs. Only parts of the building were still being used in the late nineteenth century and reports that two skulls sat on a window ledge in a nearly forgotten room give proof to the tale. Eventually, Dr. Watson, the Bishop of Llandaff who seized the property, ordered for the skulls to be boxed up and encased within the walls. An exorcism was performed to hopefully rid the house of the ghostly shenanigans, but locals still reported seeing odd lights and strange sounds coming from the once great Calgarth Hall. The house is quiet today, the coat of arms of the murderous Phillipson family still visible over one of the old fireplaces: a reminder that the past is never completely put to rest.

THE SCREAMING SKULL OF CHILTON CANTELO

The dark days of the English Civil War reached far beyond the constraints of the living. The deeds carried out by the Royalist movement convinced Theophilus Broome that after his death, his head would be in danger of being impaled on a spike as a warning. Once a follower of Charles I, he was appalled by the bloodthirsty acts committed against his countrymen and defected to the Roundhead cause. As a traitor, he knew that if discovered, he would be used as an example to others to not cross the king. Years later, Broome lay upon his deathbed with an odd request, making his sister promise to bury his body without his head and keep it safe at home. He died at the age of sixty-nine in 1670. She did as he asked, and the skull was separated from his body and remained at their shared cottage.

After she died, the house changed hands with the requirement that the skull remain. All attempts to remove the head were met with a loud protest from the head, driving many of the homeowners away with a warning for the next tenants. Finally, one man decided to contact the church and have the skull returned to its body, believing that would end the disturbances. As the sexton began to dig up the old grave, his spade broke in half, convincing him it was a bad omen. He refused to continue so the skull remained at its former home. In 1826, repairs were being made to the house when one of the workmen discovered the skull in a cupboard. Deciding it would be an appropriate cup for either tea or beer, he claimed it as his own mug until the work was finished. The skull never complained.

The skull now rests in a cabinet opposite the front door of the cottage and is looked after by the current tenants.

TUNSTEAD FARM

What do a centuries-old skull, failed railroad bridge construction, and questionable poetry have in common? They center on the legend of the Tunstead Farm skull, affectionately known as "Dickie." Hidden away in the hamlet of Chapel-en-le-Frith in Derbyshire, England, is thought to be the head of a former owner of the farm, Ned Dixon. Known as Dickie's Farm due to the history of paranormal activity that originated at the large stone house, the legend began with two stories of a murder and an unwavering attachment to the skull's last home.

The first story of the skull's presence revolved around two sisters, each of whom loved the same man as well as Tunstead Farm and possessed an unwillingness to give either up. As the family drama evolved into violence, one sister fell to the other, but before her death she swore that she would never rest away from the farm. Sidney Oldall Addy wrote of the legend in 1895 in his book *Household Tales with Other Traditional Remains, Collected in the Counties of York, Lincoln, Derby, and Nottingham*, "And so it happens that her bones are kept in a 'cheese-fat' in the farmhouse which stands in a staircase window. If the bones are removed from the vat trouble comes upon the house, strange noises are heard at night, the cattle die or are seized with illness."

In the other legend, Ned Dixson arrived home after fighting in the English Civil War to find that reports of his death were a bit misconstrued. His cousin and wife had married, keeping the farm and unwilling to relinquish control of the property to Dixson just because he was breathing. After the pair killed Dixson, the farm suffered through strange times: failed crops, loud moaning throughout the home, and the frequent appearance of a spirit. Turning to a local witch, they were advised to dig up the body and return the skull to the house in order to quiet the ghost. Satisfied, the ghost allowed the house to remain peaceful for a number of years and become its unofficial guardian.

Any attempt to move the skull from the house resulted in terrifying screams and loud knocking on the walls, though it did contribute to running the farm in other ways. It is rumored to warn of strangers stepping onto the land or the outbuildings. Knocks and raps would also accompany the birth of farm animals, alerting the farmers when they were needed to assist the livestock.

As the skull shifted from male to female in legend, one story associates it with a female ghost. Early in the nineteenth century, a tenant named Mr. Lomax told of a night when he was sitting by the kitchen fire with his infant daughter in her nearby cradle. He watched as a woman's figure descended the stairs and crossed the room to bend over the child. Thinking it was a new servant, he began to speak to her, only to watch as she disappeared. Days later, his daughter died.

In 1863, Dickie seemingly forced the Northwestern Railway Company to divert its plans to link Buxton with Whaley Bridge, crossing what became known as "Dickie's Land." Large sections of the foundation crumbled on more than one occasion, with the sections of the bridge collapsing and burying equipment. Eventually the railway company gave up and moved the line farther north. As news spread of the skull's efforts to protect its land from what it felt were invaders, the story influenced poet Samuel Laycock to write to the spirit in the *Buxton Advertiser* in 1870:

> Neaw, Dickie, be quiet wi' thee, lad,
> An' let navvies an' railways a be;
> Mon, tha shouldn't do soa,—it's to' bad,
> What harm are they doin' to thee?
> Deod folk shouldn't meddle at o',
> But leov o' these matters to th' wick;
> They'll see they're done gradeley, aw know—
> Dos' t' yer what aw say to thee, Dick?

Although content to sit in its window seat in the upper bedroom for decades, on occasion the skull left its perch by the hands of squeamish tenants of Tunstead Farm. It was once thrown into the Coombes Reservoir, and then twice buried at the church in Chapel-en-le-Frith. Each time, storms erupted over the village. Dickie was also blamed for cattle becoming sick and dying if the head had been removed. When the skull was recovered and placed back on its ledge, peace was restored.

Today, there are rumors of Dickie being once again tossed out on his ear. Will the revengeful skull of Tunstead Farm return to its former home and protect its property, or has it finally found peace and is content to remain still for the first time in centuries? Only Dickie knows for sure.

TUMBLING COFFINS

Talk about your restless dead. Sturdy wooden or metal coffins meant to embrace the remains of the dead aren't usually prone to being tossed around, yet there are reports from several places around the world of them trying to make a break for it. To date, there is still no reasonable explanation for their antics. Flooding has been ruled out in the following stories due to the lack of disturbance to the vault floor, while other vaults are high above sea level. Minor earthquakes that could have shaken them loose from their perch did not disturb other vaults in the same area of the cemeteries. So what's the common thread? It may be the anguished theme of suicide.

The Chase Crypt

The prosperity of wealthy nineteenth-century plantation owners in the West Indies led to the construction of elaborate mausoleums. The Walrond family originally built what is now known as the Chase Crypt, in Christchurch, Barbados. Partially burrowed into the ground, walls of coral, concrete, and stone protected the vault from future storms that may rage outside, though they did little to defend the future inhabitants from the tempest that was to come. An enormous slab of marble covering the entrance guarded the only way into the tomb and stood waiting for the crypt's first occupant.

In 1808, the crypt was sold to Colonel Thomas Chase, a man with a reputation for cruelty to both his family and his slaves. A relative of Chase's, Thomasina Goddard, was buried there first in a wooden coffin. Soon afterward, Chase's two-year-old daughter, Mary Anna, was laid to rest in February 1808, the victim of disease. Four years later, Mary Anna's older sister, Dorcas, was interred after her death. Rumors bled into the close-knit community that Dorcas had starved herself in response to her father's brutality. Not long afterward, a man working on the tomb opened the heavy door to find Mary Anna's small coffin standing on its head in a corner. Though there was no sign of anyone disturbing the slab outside, the outraged family immediately assumed it was a prank. Righting the coffin to its former place, they replaced the marble door and moved on.

Colonel Chase's body followed Dorcas's into the crypt after his death a few weeks later. After pulling aside the heavy door, they were horrified to discover the three coffins, previously resting on their backs, thrown around the 12-by 6-foot chamber. Placing Chase's 240-pound lead coffin inside, they righted the other coffins, placing Mary Anna's on top of one of the larger caskets and replaced the marble slab, sealing it with concrete to guard against any more attempts at vandalism or grave robbery.

Outwardly, the Chase Crypt was not disturbed again until 1816, when the bodies of young Samuel Brewster Ames in September and Samuel Brewster in November joined their family. In both cases, the coffins were found tumbled onto the floor, though the sand below them was not moved.

The islanders began to whisper of "duppies" or evil spirits. Was the family reacting to the presence of Chase and wanted to be as far away as possible, or did the restless spirit of Dorcas create such a force that the pain of her suicide manifested in the ability to move such heavy caskets? Fear began to grip the imagination of a culture firmly rooted in superstition.

When the next burial occurred in July 1819, the English governor of Barbados, Lord Combermere, was there with his wife and others to inspect the tomb. The giant slab of marble was pulled back to reveal the coffins again thrown around the small enclosure. Mrs. Combermere wrote later in her notes:

"In my husband's presence, every part of the floor was sounded to ascertain that no subterranean passage or entrance was concealed. It was found to be perfectly firm and solid; no crack was even apparent. The walls, when examined, proved to be perfectly secure. No fracture was visible, and the sides, together with the roof and flooring, presented a structure so solid as if formed of entire slabs of stone. The displaced coffins were rearranged, the new tenant of that dreary abode was deposited, and when the mourners retired with the funeral procession, the floor was sanded with fine white sand in the presence of Lord Combermere and the assembled crowd. The door was slid into its wonted position and, with the utmost care, the new mortar was laid on so as to secure it. When the masons had completed their task, the Governor made several impressions in the mixture with his own seal, and many of those attending added various private marks in the wet mortar..."

Nine months later, the seal was broken on the orders of Combermere. Hundreds of witnesses arrived to see if the coffins were once again askew. As the slab was removed, few were surprised to see that the Chase family coffins had been thrown around the chamber. The lead casket containing the body of Dorcas greeted them as it leaned against the door. Some coffins were moved so violently that gashes were present in the stone wall where it had hit before landing in the soft undisturbed sand below.

"...I examined the walls, the arch, and every part of the Vault, and found every part old and similar; and a mason in my presence struck every part of the bottom with his hammer, and all was solid. I confess myself at a loss to account for the movements of these leaden coffins. Thieves certainly had no hand in it; and as for any practical wit or hoax, too many were requisite to be trusted with the secret for it to remain unknown; and as for negroes having anything to do with it, their superstitious fear of the dead and everything belonging to them precludes any idea of the kind. All I know is that it happened and that I was an eye-witness of the fact..." The Honorable Nathan Lucas, April 18th, 1820.

The family had had enough of the notoriety from Dorcas, ordering the coffins to be removed and reburied other areas of the cemetery. The Chase Crypt remains empty today with no other paranormal activity reported.

Buxhowden

On the island of Oesel, now known as Saaremaa, in the Baltic Sea sits the crypt of the Buxhowden (also spelled Boxhoewden) family. Crashes from deep within the tomb in 1844 were reportedly loud enough to spook horses tethered nearby. As the noises continued, the authorities opened the crypt. Inside, they found coffins jumbled on the floor, one even resting on top of another, though three of the caskets were in place: the body of an old woman and two young children. To prevent another similar incident, iron racks were bolted to the walls and the wandering caskets firmly wedged into place. Ash was then scattered on the floor to catch footsteps and the door locked and sealed to protect the crypt against any further tomfoolery from outside sources.

Villagers became convinced that the Devil had his hand in making the dead dance because only those who were the least corrupted stayed still. The woman had been a devoutly religious person before her death and the children were too young. The townspeople demanded a commission to investigate the haunted caskets and rid the town of this nuisance, but before their findings were finished, another Buxhowden had died and needed to be buried. Breaking the seal, the men opened the door to reveal the same coffins strewn about the small crypt, some upside down and leaning against the stone walls, while the ash was undisturbed. Spying one coffin with its lid appearing to have been forced open, they saw an arm escaping its casket. The body had belonged to a man who had committed suicide by slitting his own throat with a razor—and the blade was now clutched in his hand, according to the men. Suicides were not permitted to buried within church grounds; the family had hoped to have him interred without further questioning of how he had died, though it appeared to have met with a bit of resistance from the other occupants of the crypt. The bodies were placed into new coffins and reburied separately, and the tomb has remained quiet ever since.

THE CATACOMBS OF PARIS: THE EMPIRE OF THE DEAD

It's hard to imagine there wouldn't be a few ghosts roaming the miles of tunnels beneath Paris in its famed catacombs. Visitors to the tomb have reported feelings of being watched or followed, and even having the sensation of being strangled. Shadowy figures dart between the stacks of bones, perhaps reluctant to give up the ghost.

How did this incredible monument to fate evolve? Its history stretches back to the open-air limestone quarries dug by the Romans in 60 BCE on the outskirts of Paris. As the need for more building material was required, crews tunneled deep underground. In 1180, a network of tunnels was used as a source for material to fortify the city until the late eighteenth century, when the weight of the city resulted in the collapse of some of the tunnels, forcing their closure.

Paris had another problem, however. Before the rise of Christianity, the city buried their dead on the outskirts of town, protecting residents from disease and the smell of rot. As the church rose to prominence, parishioners were buried within the churchyards and within the confines of city cemeteries. The *Cimetieres des Innocents* (Cemetery of the Innocent) at one time held more than thirty generations of the city's dead. Paris was running out of room.

Since a portion of the church's income came from housing the dead, they didn't turn away the bodies that arrived at their door for burial. As the land was quickly spoken for in the smaller churchyards, large pits were dug to bury the bodies of those who could not afford a private burial plot and were instead placed into mass graves by the twelfth century. When one pit was full, another would be dug close by and then filled in as well. At the Cemetery of the Innocent, the bodies piled up until the ground was said to have been over ten feet over the road. Unable to bear the weight of the soil as the mass graves swelled, the walls of some cemeteries eventually crumbled, exposing bodies as they tumbled onto the street below. Disease swept through the neighborhoods as rotten bodies poisoned the nearby well water and vermin took advantage of the grisly remains for their meals. As the living died as a result of their proximity of the overflowing cemeteries, the city had to decide what to do with the bodies.

In 1786, officials decided to move the bones—all of them—to the abandoned quarries that crisscrossed the nether regions of the city. The bones were removed from their mass graves beginning in April of that year. Always under the cover of night and accompanied by a procession of priests who sang the burial service, they walked behind the tipcarts carrying the veiled bones. It took two years to move generations of Parisian remains.

Early on, the catacombs became a macabre tourist spot for the curious. Lord d'Artois, who was later crowned Charles X, accompanied by ladies of the court, visited the tombs in 1787. At first a convenient spot to deposit the bones, the catacombs were organized in 1810 under the eye of Louis Etienne Hericart de Thury. After the walls were lined with artistically designed arches and symbols along with any cemetery decorations he could find at the original graveyard, the caverns became a showplace. As the place became the fuel for nightmares, Francois I of Austria and Napoleon III, as well as scores of Parisians, braved the damp tunnels to see the remains.

After a brief period of reconstruction in 2005, the catacombs are again open for tours. Visitors may wander the tunnels and wait for the past to greet them face to face as they enter the tunnels to be greeted by a sign reading, *Arrete! C'est ici L'Empire de la Mort*—"Stop! Here is the Empire of the Dead." You can't say you weren't warned.

FOUR

HAUNTED HOUSEKEEPING AND FRIGHTENING FURNITURE

The stuff we have in our homes tells a lot about what we feel is important. Whether our space is cluttered or magazine-layout sparse, the furniture and collectibles we choose to display reveal a glimpse into who we are and what we feel is special—even if those items have a life of their own. A glimpse of the past through a haunted mirror or the residual scream of a voice long dead emanating from a suit of armor forces us to remember that they too shared our space. For that painstaking moment, we pause to acknowledge someone whose memory has faded. Science hasn't been able to discern what's behind the mystery so we watch … and wait.

Many of our collectibles are tangible memories of those we've loved or have had a connection with either through family or location. As ghosts do their cosmic shuffle, the possibility of a last goodbye through the photograph of a beloved child or strains of music heard throughout an ancient manor house reveals that we are never quite as alone as we think. Some ghosts aren't shy about making their displeasure known if their chosen object is moved from a favorite spot. Sometimes other ghosts linger and wait for their moment to be remembered—perhaps not realizing that it's time to say goodbye.

LOVE NEVER FADES

While most vortexes and orbs can be scientifically explained away, what about the small percentage of phenomena that can't be blamed on sun glare or a photobombing bug? What if you felt your loved one was trying to communicate to you through the photograph itself? I met Todd and Theresa Apple during an event in Winchester, Virginia, in October 2012. As my paranormal investigative partner and I described the basics of ghost hunting to the crowd, the couple and their two children stood out among the rest while we went over the procedures and attempted to capture any electronic voice phenomena in the small eighteenth-century cabin. Interested, intelligent, and no-nonsense when they told me their story about their daughter, Veronica, who had passed away after surgical complications due to congenital heart defects, I knew they were absolutely sincere.

This is the portrait of Veronica Apple in which her mother saw her lips moving. Courtesy of Theresa Apple.

"Veronica died on 16 August 1997 in Baltimore, Maryland, at Johns Hopkins Hospital. She was three and a half. No one thought she would die. In fact, the day before, the doctors had told Todd that she was getting better and they were hoping to move her that weekend to a private room and out of the ICU ward. The hospital had missed a fatal infection that originated in a catheter line, and Nica died from pseudomonas sepsis. We still don't know how we managed to drive home to Sterling, Virginia, which is at least a seventy- to eighty-mile drive. We remember none of that drive," her mother Theresa said.

"We were in shock, obviously, and after making a couple of calls to advise friends and family, we sat down on the entryway steps in our foyer. We knew family would be coming, but most of them lived in California, so it would be hours before they would arrive. At that time, the picture was hanging on the landing to the upstairs level of the townhouse. Three strange things happened within a short space of time. The first has to do with the portrait. We looked over—both of us—and we could see the lips moving. Neither of us could make out what was being said, but it was very clear that Nica was trying to speak to us and tell us something. Granted, we were exhausted and in shock, but we're not overly emotional people, we're both very levelheaded, and we're not particularly inclined to seeing things that aren't there. This continued for some time, maybe a period of about a half hour. It was just us present in the room. Strangely, the phone did not ring during that period, even though we had been getting a lot of calls from people as they heard the news. It stopped about the time we decided to walk to the local store to get some laundry detergent to get the stains and smell out of our clothes from the procedures that had been done.

"The second thing occurred when we returned from the store and were sitting on our stoop. A blue jay appeared right in front of us. The bird's color was almost the same as the color of the denim dress Nica wears in the picture. We had seen cardinals in the area before, but never a blue jay. It hopped right in front of us, and came pretty close before flying off.

"The third event occurred on the day we buried Nica. She loved water and was always asking for water, yet she was denied water a lot due to her medications. Despite a very long dry spell in the area, the day we buried her, as the two of us stood alone by her graveside as they lowered her in, it started raining. Coincidence, maybe."

There has been no further activity with the picture since those first painful days. They feel the photograph may have been her way of saying farewell to the parents who cherish her still.

SAWSTON HALL AND THE GHOST OF BLOODY MARY

Politics today pale in comparison to the tomfoolery Tudor England endured. After the death of King Henry VIII in 1547, his young son, Edward VI, ascended to the throne with the overly enthusiastic help of his uncle, Edward Seymour, Duke of Somerset, and then to his successor after an unfortunate parting of Seymour's head from his neck, by John Dudley, Duke of Northumberland. As the older men jockeyed for position within the court, young Edward's half-sisters, the princesses Mary and Elizabeth, kept one foot in England and the other ready to flee the executioner's axe.

Edward VI fell ill at the age of fifteen and Dudley saw his chance to gain power. As tuberculosis invaded Edward's body, Dudley persuaded the teenaged king to name his successor as ruler to Edward's cousin—and Dudley's new daughter-in-law—Jane Grey. Convinced that his half-sister Mary, as a Catholic, would lead the country to ruin, Edward agreed. After the king's death, Dudley quickly installed Jane and his son, Guildford Dudley, as the monarchs of Great Britain. He was left in a pickle, however, regarding what to do with Mary and Elizabeth. They had legitimate claim to the throne as sisters to the king, and their supporters could become troublesome. Dudley decided to take preemptive action and dispose of the girls before they could foil his plans.

Sending a message that the young king was failing, Dudley summoned Mary and Elizabeth to the castle, hoping to imprison—and then behead—them both with a minimum of fuss. Elizabeth, the sharper of the two, sensed a trap and refused to come. Mary, seeing her own future as queen within her grasp, immediately set out for London.

As the princess got closer to the capital, she received word of Dudley's betrayal. Taking refuge with her friends the Huddlestons at Sawston Hall near Cambridge, Mary rested in the Tapestry Room and waited. Dudley had sent his son Robert with three hundred men to capture and return the princess. As dawn broke, a guard atop the roof at Sawston sounded the alarm to rouse the family and take action. Disguising Mary as a maid, Sir John Huddleston took the rightful queen from the house, having her ride behind one of his grooms. Escaping before the cavalry descended upon the Hall, they watched as the troops burned the structure. Mary vowed to return the house to its former glory to repay the Huddlestons for their kindness once she was installed as queen.

Mary returned to London on her own terms and disposed of John Dudley the Duke of Northumberland. Lady Jane Grey and her husband Guildford Dudley were also beheaded so there would be no further claim upon the throne or risk of Grey's supporters coming to arms against her. Bloody Mary had begun her reign with swift vengeance.

The Tapestry Bedroom, so called for the set of Flemish tapestries that hang on the walls of the bedroom and where Mary spent her restless night, features a large four-poster bed that had been spared the flames that destroyed other portions of the house. The legend states that when people spend the night in the room, some will hear three slow knocks upon the heavy door, then the door opens and a woman in gray floats across the room and into a tapestry.

The bed, reported to have been the one Mary had used, is the one she frequently visits when making her ghostly rounds. Hearing heavy breathing coming from an unknown source beside her awaked one woman sleeping in the bed, while later, a man was awoken after hearing knocking on the door and a furious rattling of the latches. Neither was eager to sleep in that room again.

British researcher Hans Holzer spent the night in the haunted bed hoping to learn more about the restless ghost. Setting his clock for seven in the morning, he was awakened with the alarm went off at 4 a.m., 5 a.m., and again at 6 a.m. Each time, the sound alerted him to door latch being lifted as if someone were about to enter the room. He felt that the presence was more protective than alarming.

Mary was also a talented pianist before her death during the influenza epidemic of 1558. Is the music heard occasionally throughout the Hall a residual haunting of her playing an ancient virginal?

BRIDAL RAGE

Baker Mansion, now home to the Blair County Historical Society in Altoona, Pennsylvania, houses a ghost with anger-management issues. Elias Baker and his family moved to the area after co-purchasing the Allegheny Furnace with Baker's cousin, Roland Diller, in 1836. Moving from a "tolerable good mansion house," after buying out Diller in 1844, Baker contracted Robert Cary Long Jr. to design a grander home to show off the great wealth he'd made as an iron baron. Work began on the three-story, twenty-eight-room, Greek Revival mansion with six enormous fluted Ionic columns gracing the front deck in 1845, but due to complications, the house wasn't completed until 1849.

During that time, Baker raised his children, David Woods, Sylvester, and Anna, with his wife, Hetty. Anna grew into adulthood, and as the daughter of a prosperous man, she had her pick of eligible suitors. Naturally, she fell in love with, according to her father, the wrong man. Elias Baker forbade her from marrying a steelworker from the furnace. Anna then vowed to never marry and remained a spinster. She cared for her brother Sylvester in their home until her death in 1914.

After the Baker County Historical Society assumed possession of the grand house, a wedding dress worn by Elizabeth Dysart Bell—a prominent businessman's daughter who reportedly wore the same dress Anna had chosen for her own nuptials—was put on display under a glass case in Anna's bedroom. Legend has it that visitors and museum staff have seen the dress gently sway or violently shake within its case on nights when the moon is full. The parasol and shoes also on display in the case have also been reported to change positions. The dress has since been removed and packed safely away to prevent further deterioration.

Anna's fit of jealousy isn't the only paranormal activity in the mansion. Her brother, Sylvester, has also been seen roaming the hallways, his cane tapping along the floor and feet stomping, and what they believe may be Anna herself has been sighted in the parlor and second-floor bedrooms. Cellars are creepy enough, but there are reports of hearing screams coming from the ice room where the body of Anna's brother, David Woods, was stored during the cold months of 1852 after his death in a steamboat accident. The ground being too frozen to break for burial, the family kept David close by until the spring thaw. It may have been a little too close, however, as strange thumping and banging noises have been rising from the cellar. Mirrors have been said to reflect ghostly figures and a music box plays a simple tune, its wheel turning as if cranked by an invisible hand. I wonder if it's the wedding march for poor Anna.

YOU CAN'T KEEP AN OLD GIRL DOWN

Snug against a bend in the James River in southern Virginia sits the eighteenth-century colonial mansion Shirley Plantation. Part of the early years of the English colony, the settlement of the land by Thomas West began in 1613 for tobacco cultivation, six years after the landing of ships at nearby Jamestown and seven years before pilgrims bumped into Plymouth Rock. Passed down in 1638 to Edward Hill I, a farm was built and secured the land for future generations. Construction of the Great House began in 1723 by Edward Hill III upon his daughter Elizabeth's marriage to John Carter, the eldest son of the influential and wealthy Robert "King" Carter. It took fifteen years to complete the mansion, as no cost was spared in its construction to last the ages.

Many of the original furnishings are kept within the building as the Shirley Plantation is still owned, operated, and lived in by descendants of Edward Hill I, making it the oldest family-owned business in North America. The impressive three-story, brick Great House has stood through Indian attacks, Bacon's Rebellion, the American Revolution, and the Civil War with style, grace, and at least one persnickety ghost. At the time of the Civil War, the house was used as a field hospital as General McClellan transported over 8,000 injured and dying men out of Virginia by using Shirley Plantation's close proximity to the James River as a way to move the men onto ships and back over Union lines.

Within the collection of family portraits hangs a picture of a woman with lovely brown hair pulled back from her face in soft waves and displaying a strong jaw. Her dark eyes seem to stare directly at the viewer, though not as an invitation to learn more about her but to warn them against the intrusion. It is believed the portrait is of a sister or daughter of Edward Hill III, Martha. Martha left for England to study and subsequently marry, while the painting remained at Shirley in an upstairs bedroom for years. Eventually the portrait became known as "Aunt Pratt." While the rooms were being remodeled a generation later, her portrait was taken down and stored in the attic.

Aunt Pratt didn't like to be ignored. Soon, sounds, described by the family as a "mighty disturbance" in the form of a chair being rocked furiously, came from the attic. This continued until the painting was once again hung in its former bedroom chamber. The noises ceased…for a time.

During a tourism promotion of items with supernatural phenomena in the 1970s, the Virginia Travel Council picked up on the stories of Aunt Pratt's antics and borrowed it for an exhibition at Rockefeller Plaza in New

York City. Hung in a display case, the portrait started to swing, according to witnesses, moving back and forth so wildly that the seal of Virginia, which had been hung beside it, also began to rock. On his way to lunch, a reporter from NBC stopped by to the see the exhibit and caught the painting making a commotion on tape, giving the portrait and its story national coverage. One morning, workmen in the building discovered the painting lying on the floor several feet away from its display case, describing the scene as if Aunt Pratt was "heading toward the exit."

After that, the wandering painting was locked in a closet when not on exhibition. However, the maintenance crew reported hearing knocking and crying coming from the closet while they worked at night. The next morning, Aunt Pratt's portrait was found outside of the small room. After calling in psychic experts, it was theorized that there were two spirits associated with the painting: one portrait had been painted over another and one of the ladies was quite put out by the imposition.

The portrait of Aunt Pratt returned to Virginia by way of Richmond to have its frame repaired after its adventure. When the portrait was retrieved by the family, the shop owner told them he had heard bells while the picture was in his care. No bells were discovered in his shop, so he assumed Pratt had been up to her old tricks. The painting was once again hung in its favorite spot and no other occurrences have been reported.

THE BLUSHING PORTRAIT

Tucked away outside of Richmond, Virginia, in the hamlet of Amelia, sits a plantation rich in history and harboring more than a few mysteries. Built in 1745, the estate nestled within its 15,000 acres is a large and imposing mansion with plentiful gardens, multiple outbuildings, slave quarters, and two graveyards: one for family and one for their slaves. After the American Civil War ravaged the countryside, the estate never regained its full glory and fell into a dismal state as it passed from owner to owner. With no one able to keep up with the demands of such a large house and grounds, Haw Branch Plantation became the token creepy place to avoid in the once-prosperous area.

In 1964, Haw Branch once again changed hands, but this time to a couple who wouldn't be so easily put off by stories of strange disturbances and the occasional sound of a body falling into their dry moat. Cary and Gibson McConnaughey immediately began to renovate the property that had sat vacant for fifty years after the death of Mrs. McConnaughey's grandmother, a former owner. With the house in need of serious repair, its enormous chimneys requiring immediate restoration and acres of fields to be tended to, it took years of hard work to bring the plantation back to life.

After moving their two children and two dogs into the large manor home, all was quiet—at first. Approximately three months after they finally made the house their own, paranormal activity began terrifying the family. Footsteps fell on quiet floors at night, and the distinct smell of oranges and roses wafted throughout the house. Visions of a man walking out of the barn holding a lantern were seen along with another man pleading for help and a third fellow walking with a limp. However, these apparitions are just a side note to what happened the night of November 23, 1965. Deep in sleep, the McConnaugheys were jolted from their rest as screams ripped through the house. They found their children on the landing, staring up at the attic stairs as the sound continued. No one, not even the dog baring its teeth to protect its family, would ascend the steps to see what was trapped behind the attic door.

Sounds continued to frequent the house: heavy items being dropped, a rocking chair was heard slowly gliding away the hours, and furniture was often heard being drug across the attic floor. Six months later on May 23, the family was again awakened by the horrified screams of the woman in the attic. The screams were repeated every six months until they were replaced by an entity seen by Mrs. McConnaughey in 1967. E. Randall Floyd, in his book

More Great Southern Mysteries, quoted the homeowner as saying, "I could plainly see the silhouette of a slim girl in a floor-length dress with a full skirt." She continued, "I could see no features, but she was not transparent, just a white silhouette." Mrs. McConnaughey saw the ghost several more times, as did her daughter, who woke up to find the woman in white standing over her bed as she slept.

However, the oddest phenomenon was yet to come. An elderly cousin was delighted the family had taken on the challenge of Haw Branch. Sending a portrait of a distant relative named Florence Wright, their cousin had described the painting as a beautiful pastel, drawn right before the tragic early death of their ancestress from a stroke. Eagerly opening the crate that held the portrait after it arrived, the family was disappointed to find it not quite as their cousin had described. Instead of vibrant, brilliant colors, the painting was of a woman crudely drawn in a mix of black, grays, and dingy whites.

Instead of hiding it behind the sofa, they placed it over the fireplace mantel in the library. Days later, the voices began. Mrs. McConnaughey, hearing women speaking to her from the library while she was in another part of the house, rushed to greet her visitors only to find an empty room. The disembodied voices continued to taunt the family, until one day while reading in the library, Mr. McConnaughey discovered that the portrait of Florence was tinged with color. Amazed, they watched as over a period of a year and a half, the painting slowly filled with shades of green and red; Florence revealed herself to be a stunning redhead with eyes the color of the blue sky as she sat on a green chair next to a pale-green vase with a pink rose. At some angles, it appeared the woman in the painting would blush as you looked at her, but in other light, it looked as if the portrait was bleeding. Experts were brought in from local colleges to examine the portrait and explain the mystery behind the sudden change in hues, but no one was able to give a firm and logical answer, leaving the painting and the secrets of Haw Branch Plantation quiet at last.

CHAIR OF DOOM

What's that tingle? Patrons of the Busby Stoop Inn, located in Kirby Wiske in North Yorkshire, Great Britain, could count on a few things while stopping for the night: a good story, warm ale, and a fair chance of dying horribly if you sat in a particular chair. In 1702, Thomas Busby and his father-in-law, Daniel Awety, were in cahoots to rob the crown of its full weight of gold by shaving coins to make counterfeits. A notorious drunkard with a short temper, Busby overreacted to the sight of Awety sitting in his favorite chair at a pub after an argument over business. Bludgeoning the man to death with a hammer later that night at Awety's home, Busby dragged the body into nearby woodland. When Awety failed to show up for breakfast the next day, a search ensued and the corpse was discovered.

Busby was arrested for the murder, tried, and condemned to hang soon after with his corpse slated to occupy a hanging iron cage as a warning to others who thought of foul deeds. Before his hanging, Busby was heard to curse anyone who dared to sit in his chair to die a cruel death. Since that time, his ghost has been reported to have been seen, noose hanging limply from his broken neck, near the site of his hanging. The chair remained in the pub and the legend grew. Locals would dare each other to test their fate against the dead man's chair until a slew of accidents made them pause and wonder if, indeed, Busby had had his revenge.

Late in the eighteenth century, a chimney sweep who had sat in the chair the evening before was found hanging from a gatepost near Busby's former perch. Years later, airmen who had visited and encouraged each other to sit in the chair both died from injuries incurred from a car crash the same day. More deaths followed as reports of several bicyclists and motorists were involved in fatal crashes soon after sitting in the chair. After a young man working as a laborer fell through the roof after resting in the chair earlier that day in the late nineteenth century, the pub owner locked the chair away in the cellar. Donating the cursed chair to the Thirsk Museum, he made the museum promise to never again let anyone sit in the chair, and it has now hung from a museum wall for over thirty years.

OLD SPARKY

Charming, capricious, and deadly, the world's first man to be identified as a serial killer by the United States Federal Bureau of Investigation met his death still convinced he could persuade the courts that they couldn't prove a thing. Theodore "Ted" Robert Bundy terrorized a nation as young women were kidnapped, raped, and murdered between the years of 1974 to 1978, totaling over thirty deaths across six states. However, it was believed Bundy started his killing spree at as a young teenager and was said to be responsible for the disappearance of his eight-year-old neighbor Ann Marie Burr in 1961, while living with his family in Washington state.

With an easygoing charade of charisma and intelligence, Bundy graduated from the University of Washington and attended the University of Washington Law School while working as a crisis hotline counselor alongside future true crime writer Ann Rule and campaigning for the U.S. Republican Party. Well-educated and liked by many, he never showed any hints of the rage that burned inside. In his normalcy lay the real danger.

A handsome man with no outwardly sign of menace, Bundy would lure victims into his car with stories of needing help while displaying an injured arm before he proceeded to kill, then rape and sodomize their bodies, often hiding them stacked in the vast forests of Washington so he could visit them again.

Initially apprehended in 1975 in Utah, Bundy escaped from prison several times until he was finally caught for good and secured in Florida in 1978. He was convicted of the murder of a twelve-year-old girl, though it was suspected that he had a hand in the death of over a hundred women across the United States. As his story spread, his notoriety fed his ego and he called upon his years in law school to help him defend himself in court. After dragging out the trial with legal technicalities and promises of showing authorities where other bodies had been buried, Bundy's string of luck finally ran out, and he faced death by the electric chair, nicknamed "Old Sparky" by the Florida State Prison in Redford, Florida.

His head shaved and his last meal eaten, Bundy was led to the execution chamber where he said his final words to the small group of witnesses: "I'd like you to give my love to my family and friends." Strapped into the wooden chair, he waited. At 7:16 a.m. on January 24, 1989, the executioner pulled the switch and Bundy's manipulation over of his madness was finished.

In 2001, a former guard from the prison told a Tampa-area newspaper reporter that he and other guards had witnessed Bundy's ghost reclining in the electric chair that had ended his life. Described as acknowledging them with a "knowing smile," this haunting faded as they approached the entity. The guard continued his story, saying that there were so many sightings of the mass murderer that many of the guards refused to enter the execution chamber alone. Bundy also frequented the small cell on the prison's death row. As guards entered the room, some would hear him say, "Well, I beat all of you, didn't I?" Did he mean he'd cheated them by not revealing where more bodies were hidden or that he had reached the other side first?

Prison officials are rumored to have threatened staff with dismissal if stories of Bundy's ghost appeared in public. As guards quit after seeing Bundy's ghost on its haunted electric chair, they didn't require the warning—they were long gone.

As much as Bundy liked to travel the United States while alive, his ghost may also have itchy feet. An entity recognized as the killer has been seen around the Chi Omega sorority house where he committed two murders, as well as being seen on the porch of a building in Tallahassee, Tennessee, where he had laid low between killings. Bundy's remains were cremated and scattered in the vast forest of Washington state. Mixing with the wind and rain, his ashes may rest over the bodies of nameless victims he'd buried in those same woods.

BELCOURT CASTLE

It's not a summer in Rhode Island until your getaway cottage boasts a shrieking suit of armor. The construction of Belcourt Castle, in Newport, began in 1891, taking over three years and three hundred craftsmen to complete the massive Louis XIII–style structure. Oliver Hazard Perry Belmont (son of the man for whom the Belmont Stakes were named) patterned the house after a hunting lodge at Versailles, filling the cavernous rooms with antiques, medieval manuscripts, and an extensive collection of horse-related items at a cost of $3.2 million dollars in 1894 (over $80 million dollars in 2013).

Though the original plans for the house designed by famed architect Richard Morris Hunt called for sixty rooms, only one traditional bedroom and bathroom were completed. No kitchen or guest rooms were included, and meals were brought in by carriage from town. As a summer retreat, Belmont reasoned that there would be no call for adding on rooms he would never use, so he put the space to better use for storing his collections. On the ground floor, the structure housed an eccentric display of carriages and stables for horses.

In 1895, Belmont greeted his first visitors with a grand ball to signal the completion of his new home. The ball's hostess was the wife of Oliver's best friend and business partner, William Kissam Vanderbilt. A year later, Alva Erskine Smith Vanderbilt divorced her husband and married Oliver. The Belmonts traveled extensively, filling their home with unusual additions to their collection of suits of armor and other artifacts until Oliver died in 1908. After he passed away, Alva redesigned the first floor of Belcourt, evicting the horses to exterior stables; then she added a kitchen, banquet hall, library complete with hidden doors, and renovated a study into a bedroom.

As the mansion grew into old age, it watched its owners fall. Alva died in 1933, then her brother 1940. Passing out of the Belmont family, it fell into decay as the new tenants could not keep up with its demands. Saved by the Tinney family, the once-grand summer cottage of Oliver Belmont was restored when they purchased the property in 1956. Filling it with their own art and antique collections gathered from around the world, the Tinneys brought not only grandeur back into the old home, but they may have brought a few ghosts as well.

In the late 1950s, the Tinney family began giving tours of the estate. Ten years later, they began The Royal Arts Foundation to help educate the public on various antiques in their collection and the architectural style of a home from the Gilded Age of the late nineteenth century. They also began to give paranormal tours led by medium Virginia Smith to help alleviate the costs of preserving Belcourt Castle.

While in the French Gothic ballroom, visitors have described feelings of unease, an icy dip in temperature, and ripples of energy coming from a pair of antique chairs. Known as "salt chairs" for their removable seat that stores a saltcellar, it is believed that these chairs may have a royal history as there have been reports of entities resembling a French queen and king nearby. In one chair, the unseen occupant seems to repel anyone invading their space while the other chair has been rumored to toss people out of it.

A row of empty suits of armor dating to the fifteenth and sixteenth centuries stand at attention at one end of the ballroom. Every March, screams are heard echoing throughout the chamber as one of the suits of armor relives the original owner's horrible death, a spear tip piercing his head through the slit in the helmet. The helmet has also been rumored to turn by itself to follow the progression of strangers who tour the house.

A monk, dressed in a brown robe and hood, has been seen by the Tinneys and guests after they brought home a German carving of one of the brotherhood on their travels. Attached to the carving, the entity has been seen wherever it has been displayed, even once entering the first-floor ladies room. Do monks blush?

Other spirits roam the hallways of Belcourt Castle, including dancing girls seen by Donald Tinney in the haunted ballroom, a lady on the second-floor gallery in a ball gown, a British soldier in his dress uniform, and a Samurai warrior believed to have hitched a ride with the Tinney's Asian collection of antiquities. There are many accounts of items being moved or borrowed within the house, only to be returned later.

The Atlantic Paranormal Society (TAPS) team has investigated the house many times, with the *Ghost Hunters* episode originally airing on the Syfy channel on April 11, 2009. Currently, ghost tours led by Harle Tinney are available to visit the mansion and hear her fifty years of paranormal experiences.

MR. BAGABONES AND THE HAUNTED TRUNK

What if you received a nudge from beyond that solved the mystery of a missing woman? Brian McKavanagh of Toronto, Ontario, known as "Mr. Bagabones" on the Haunted Society website, shared with me his story of his neighbor and friend, Helen:

"Way back, [we] lived in this old Victorian-style house, split down [the] middle. A lady older/widow rented other side. My wife [and] her sister [were] quite friendly with her, [they] loved Helen's homemade pierogies. We both shared a big old garage with giant wooden door that lifted up to enter. [In] those days, I used [to own an] old Cadillac with the wings to go back [and] forth to work in; when [I] pulled it into [the] garage, both cars were separated by one of those sea trunks with [an] old-style latch, and owned by [the] lady next door. A keepsake from her travels to her new home Canada, as she came from Portugal.

"It's winter and my wife and her sister start nagging me. They have not seen our neighbour Helen for a week or so, or her little dog. They said her bathroom window was slightly open. I am trying to enjoy dinner and said maybe she's on holiday to Florida and left [the] window open a bit to air while she's gone. I got that look that women give us men, so I did my best and said, 'Don't worry, she'll be back.' I got that look again. My wife gets in my face and says, 'Listen! Helen is in trouble, she's crying out for help. DO SOMETHING!'

"During next week, I went faithfully to work, parked the car, got out, [and] did my routine of sitting on the trunk [and] had my smoke while taking off my snow boots before I entered the house. [I] would sit there contemplating the day's events while flicking back and forth the old broken key latch of the trunk. I was tempted to lift open [the lid of] the trunk, but it was Helen's and I respected her property. [For] some reason [I] felt compelled open it, but never did.

"[On the] last working day [of the] week, [I] came up [the] narrow alley to [the] garage and was stopped by a deluge of cop cars. Walking up to garage, I found it cornered off by [the] police and saw them pulling garbage bags out of the trunk. [I] got to my place [to] find cops and detectives questioning my wife. [It] seems my wife had had enough and phoned them to check on Helen.

"In the end, I knew something was up, but [it] did not click into [the] voice in my head that shouted to me to 'OPEN THE TRUNK!'

"Helen was killed over a financial dispute by a boyfriend she was dating. He, in the end, killed her dog and left it in basement. [He] killed her, chopped her body up in the top washroom's bathtub, and then transported her remains to the trunk in garage where she lay frozen in cold winter temperatures. [He] then proceeded to steal her Royal Doultons and jewels, but he was traced and caught before he got out of country. [The] police came back to my wife [and were] curious about how she knew about Helen's fate. Being police, they are not allowed to believe in ESP or gifted ones, but in end thanked my wife for her help in catching Helen's killer.

"Helen's cry for help was heard. She will be missed, so to those out there who take a life and think you won't be caught, you forgot about human spirit. You can't hide; it will catch up with you in this world or the other.

"I got the message Helen and told your side of the story."

THE TROUBLE WITH DUMPSTER DIVING

An antique walnut-framed mirror sold on the auction site eBay in February 2013 after a series of alleged paranormal attacks on its former owners. Plucking the mirror from their landlord's trash months before, the men who took it claimed to have been plagued by bad luck ever since. Financial problems, illness, and even feelings of doom had invaded their living space since bringing the mirror into their home.

In an interview with the British newspaper the *Daily Mail*, owner Joseph Birch described waking up with stabbing pains throughout his body and said, "When I pass the mirror, I see flickering shadows reflected in it. I would stand completely still and they continued, and I'd get quick glimpses of black darkness." Whether the mirror was truly haunted or the flatmates just wanted to get the ugly mirror out of the house, we'll never know, but for the bargain price of $155, the new owners will hopefully get what they paid for.

FIVE

OUT OF POCKET
EXPERIENCES

Some haunted things are just too big to have on a mantel-piece or fit in your pocket. The stories shared in this chapter revolve around things that may be visited, such as the road where Revolutionary War hero Mad Anthony Wayne still searches for his missing bones, the haunted Chicago River that echoes the tragedy of the Eastland Disaster, or a monument with a shady past. Each of these has a tale to tell, from my own experience at a ghost town in Montana to a woman's desperate search for home on the beach near Cape Hatteras lighthouse.

MAD ANTHONY WAYNE

A Revolutionary War hero with a quick temper and flashes of bravado isn't one to let the boiling of his bones stop him from popping in to see the living. Major General "Mad" Anthony Wayne is famous more for his death and two burial sites rather than many of his ill-conceived attacks on the enemy. A loyal friend of George Washington, he quickly rose in the ranks after enlisting in the Continental Army in the early days of the American Revolution. When he retired after the war to serve in the Pennsylvania state Legislature and as a U.S. Congressman, his exploits on and off the battlefield faded into memory until Washington called upon him once again.

Native American attacks on settlers crossing into the Northwest Territory and the pesky British to the north forced Washington to ask his friend to take charge. Washington gave him the title of Commander-in-Chief of the newly formed Legion of the United States, and Wayne organized the extension of the United States Army in 1791. After a few years of successfully squashing uprisings by Native Americans and peace treaties signed, he was on his way home to Philadelphia. Wayne's last stop was at Fort Presque Isle, now known as Erie, Pennsylvania, after a five-day sail on the sloop *Detroit*, leaving from the city that bore the same name in November 1796. While the trip itself was pleasant, Wayne's health began to bother him and his days were filled with writing letters expressing his last wishes and how they were to be carried out.

By the time he reached Fort Presque Isle, Wayne had suffered a serious attack of gout. Wayne asked for his friend, Dr. J. C. Wallace, to be brought in to help, though Wallace was one hundred miles away in Pittsburgh and the disease was slowly, and painfully, killing Wayne. In the early morning hours of December 15, 1796, Wayne passed away from complications of gout only to have Wallace arrive later that day. Reading from his letters, the company at Fort Presque Isle carried out Wayne's final wishes to be buried in full uniform within two days of his death. With him being buried in a simple wooden coffin, round-headed brass tacks were pounded into the lid to display his initials, age, and year of death. He was buried at the foot of the blockhouse's flagstaff on garrison hill as requested in his letters.

And there General Wayne's body remained, happily resting, until thirteen years later when his family remembered that it was missing from the family plot—four hundred miles away. His daughter, Margaretta, sent her younger brother Isaac to retrieve the bones and bring them back for a reburial ceremony and a rousing town party. Setting off in a small two-wheeled carriage called a sulky, Isaac arrived at Fort Presque Isle and contacted Dr.

Wallace, whom, for a large amount of cash, agreed to prepare the bones to be escorted back by the forgetful son.

Choosing not to be present when his father's body was exhumed, Isaac missed the reaction when Dr. Wallace discovered the body of the general was almost perfectly intact. With the exception of a foot and one part of a leg, General Wayne's body had been preserved by the chilly northern temperature, which resulted in a bit of a pickle. How was Isaac supposed to get a now-rapidly decomposing body home in a tiny carriage to Radnor, Pennsylvania, without attracting stray dogs?

General Wayne Stew

With the help of four hearty assistants and a gaggle of spectators, Dr. Wallace employed the Native American custom of boiling the bones to peel away the flesh, making transportation easier. One witness to the dissection wrote years later that the body wasn't hard after being in the ground all that time; it was more of the consistency of soft chalk. Another witness wrote that he was told the "the flesh on his backbone was 4 inches thick, solid and firm like new pork." Dicing the general up into manageable pieces using his surgical equipment, Wallace boiled the body parts in a large cauldron until the stringy bits of meat fell from the bones. Then, putting the bones into the box brought by Isaac for his father's remains, Dr. Wallace dumped the cooked filet of his old friend, Wayne's uniform, organ meat, the surgical tools he used in the procedure, plus a few quarts of Eau de Wayne, back into the coffin and buried it in its former hole at the base of the flagstaff. One item remained out of its grave: a boot worn by Mad Anthony Wayne was still in good working order, the other having rotted away, so it was given to an onlooker. He had a match made for the boot and wore the pair until they eventually wore out.

Packing the box into the back of the sulky, Isaac Wayne crossed the state along bumpy roads to the jostle of his horse's canter. Along the way, the box was rumored to have sprung open, causing some of General Wayne's bones to bounce out of their container and onto what is now Route 322. It was rumored that Isaac was too disturbed about the dismal way his father's remains were treated back at Fort Presque Isle to have noticed a few finger bones were missing by the time he arrived home in Radnor. Isaac made the trip in time for the reburial of the wartime hero on July 4, 1809, at St. David's Episcopal Church. Now, on the anniversary of the general's birth, January 1, his ghost can be seen roaming lonely stretches of Route 322 in search of his missing bones. With his flesh buried in one plot and his bones in another, who could blame him for being a little discombobulated?

Wayne's ghost is not content to pick through the highway litter for a stray bone, however. The general has been seen numerous places throughout the Eastern Seaboard. Frequent sightings along US Route 1 near the Brandywine battlefield at Chadds Ford, Pennsylvania, tell of his exploits riding a white stallion into a battle that occurred in September 1777, allowing Washington and his men to escape to safety after the British and German troops nearly overcame the Continental troops at the Brandywine River.

He and his horse, Nab, have also been seen as they rode to warn American troops of an impending attack in 1779 at Storm King Pass on the Hudson River. His ride through the blustery night is replayed as a residual haunting for those lucky enough to step into the loop and witness the reported orange and blue sparks made by Nab's horseshoes striking the ground. Locals swear that the appearance of the pair means a storm is brewing and to prepare for the worst.

A ladies' man, Anthony Wayne once wooed two women with regrettable consequences. Penelope Hayes, the daughter of a rich landowner in Vermont, was the unknowing competitor for his affections with Nancy Coates, a local servant woman. Wayne and Nancy became lovers, but as she tried to make the solider put a ring on it, he resisted. As the British made advances on the territory, Washington asked Wayne to bring Hayes back to Fort

Ticonderoga. While away on his mission, talk in the fort reached Nancy's ears of Wayne leaving only to bring back Hayes as his bride. Brokenhearted, she watched as they returned.

As the wagon passed, Nancy reportedly reached out to touch her lover's boot and beg for an ounce of recognition. His attention on Penelope, he didn't feel her hand. Nancy, finally accepting that he would never love her, fled to a nearby lake where she sat until dawn. As the sun broke over the trees, she walked into the deep water and ended her life. Nancy's ghost is now part of the tangle of Mad Anthony's hauntings. Witnesses have seen her spirit running along the paths twisting and turning around the lake, the sounds of her grief echoing along the dark glens until silenced by the water. Occasionally, her ghost may be seen floating face up in the lake, a grim reminder of love lost.

Wayne isn't easily rousted from the fort either. His ghost has been seen in the commandant's dining room and sitting in a wing chair by the fireplace while smoking a churchwarden pipe and having a bit of ale from a pewter mug, mimicking the portrait of General Wayne that hangs in the room.

THE *EASTLAND* DISASTER

Water is a powerful attractant for paranormal activity. The Chicago River refuses to give up the souls it gathered in the early nineteenth century in one of the worst maritime tragedies in the city's history.

Morning broke into rainy sunlight the day of the Western Electric Company's annual picnic on July 24, 1915. An early morning boarding onto the chartered passenger liner *Eastland*, and others for the event had swelled the crowd into the thousands on Wacker Drive, between the Clark and LaSalle Street bridges along the Chicago River. Anxious for a day of food, music, and sporting events, employees and their families welcomed the chance to sail on the luxury liner known as "The Greyhound of the Lakes" on their way to Michigan City, Indiana.

The *Eastland*, recently outfitted with more lifeboats after the *Titanic* disaster and the enactment of the La Follette Seaman's Act, was even more unsteady than usual. Past reports of the liner being top-heavy and listing badly enough to take in water via the gangways in 1903 had resulted in redesigning the ship, but questions remained. The new addition of lifeboats and several tons of concrete laid on the 'tween deck and the main deck to shore up the rotting wood on the decks now made the listing even more pronounced—especially when passengers crowded the upper decks. While the *Eastland* filled to her capacity of 2,572 people that morning, the ship started to rock in its watery cradle.

Excited families began to board at 6:30 a.m., and the *Eastland* started to tip toward the dock. The order was sent below for the port ballast tanks to be filled and steady the ship as more people made their way onto the decks. Ten minutes later, the Eastland was again steady. At 6:53 a.m., the ship began to tilt toward the port side and was righted by the crew, but the ship filled to capacity quickly. The ship listed once more until at 7:20 a.m., and water began to fill through openings in the lower port side of the *Eastland*. Passengers rushed to the side to watch, making the boat tip farther, apparently enjoying the sensation and not worried as they watched items slide across the deck. Another ship chartered for the picnic could be heard playing "I'm on My Way to Dear Old Dublin Bay" nearby, as the morning's impending disaster became a reality.

At 7:28 a.m., the ship had a list of 45 degrees. While passengers still crowded the port side to wave at a passing Chicago fireboat, the liner tipped completely to its side and came to rest on the river bottom, 20 feet below the surface. Some passengers were able to pull themselves to safety and stood atop the starboard hull of the great ship, ready to use a nearby tugboat, the *Kenosha*, as a bridge to the dock. Others who had been on the top deck were flung into the water and tried to stay afloat in the river's strong currents as panic overcame the scene and rescue boats rushed to pull victims from the river.

Many of the ship's early passengers had moved below to one of the three other decks to accommodate those still boarding were trapped. Furniture, including pianos, chairs, and bookcases, crushed them against each other, meaning most of the victims are believed to have died of suffocation—not drowning—though by the time the rescuers were able to reach them by cutting holes in the metal hull, those who survived the initial rollover had drowned.

Rescue efforts began immediately, though with bodies littering the water, it soon became a recovery mission. As the dead piled up along the wharf after being plucked from the river, the city decided to establish the Second Regiment Armory on Washington Boulevard as a makeshift morgue for unidentified bodies. Corpses stretched out in rows of 85 along the wet floors awaiting identification from friends and family left behind. The process of claiming the dead took a few days because 22 entire families had been killed and had no one left to bring them home.

The death toll of the disaster totaled 844 lives. This included 841 passengers, two crew members, and one rescuer from another ship chartered for the occasion who died in the effort to save others.

An inquiry into the deaths on board the *Eastland* blamed faulty ballast tanks and their inability to right the ship as capacity was reached, but others felt the addition of the lifeboats had tipped the scales, dooming an already top-heavy ship into certain failure. It wasn't a matter of "if" as much as "when."

Since the *Eastland* tragedy, paranormal activity haunts the river and the surrounding area. There have been reports of sudden large surges of water overtaking the riverwalk area of lower Wacker Drive, much like the power of the water that would have been displaced when the *Eastland* tipped over. Visitors have also reported hearing screaming and loud splashes of water by the Clarke Street Bridge but only encounter a quiet river when they check to see if anyone needed help. More disturbing are accounts of people having lunch at one of the many cafes along the walk only to find the faces of tortured souls staring back from the depths of the Chicago River.

The armory that had served as a temporary morgue where bodies were taken is also the site of a residual haunting. Currently the studio headquarters of HARPO Productions and Oprah Winfrey, visitors and employees have witnessed hearing children laughing, music, whispering voices, and heart-wrenching sobbing throughout the building, as well as an apparition they have dubbed the "Grey Lady." An army of footsteps echoes throughout the lobby staircase while doors often slam shut by unseen hands.

SHE HAUNTS THE WAVES

Did Theodosia Burr Alston leap to her death while traveling aboard the schooner *Patriot* in 1813 after being overcome by pirates or was she a victim of her own madness years later? Theodosia, or Theo as she was more commonly known, was the daughter of Aaron Burr, the vice president under Thomas Jefferson and crack shot duelist who killed Alexander Hamilton. With her boarding the *Patriot* on New Year's Eve, 1812, en route to visit her father after the death of her own young son, Theo's full story is still a mystery.

Young, beautiful, and highly accomplished, Theo was the only child of the Burrs. After her mother passed away, Theo assumed the role as hostess to her father's estate at Richmond Hall in Albany, New York, while he navigated the rough waters of politics. Devoted to Burr, Theo was an excellent companion and charmed men easily, including the man her father was to eventually kill over an argument, Hamilton. In 1880, she met and fell in love with Joseph Alston. The two were married a year later and she moved with him to South Carolina to his family plantation, "The Oaks."

As she made her home among the heat and humidity of the unfamiliar southern climate, Theo's life began to tear at the edges. A difficult labor brought their beloved son, Aaron Burr Alston, into their lives but had left her weak and unable to cope with the demands of motherhood. Depression began to cloud her days. Joseph's successful bid to become governor of South Carolina burdened her even further and her health weakened. Struggling to excel at both her family obligations and her new role as the First Lady of South Carolina, the pressure began to take its toll. As her father's political life became embroiled in scandal with the duel that left the popular former Secretary of the Treasury, Hamilton, dead, she was determined to be strong throughout his trial for murder. When he was acquitted of the crime, Burr was left resentful of those whom he'd felt had worked against him. A few years later and plotting to place himself as the head of a new nation made of states west of the Appalachian Mountains, he now faced treason charges from the United States government. Lacking any substantial evidence, the government's case fell apart and Burr was found not guilty—at least by the law. The court of public opinion, which had yet to forgive him for killing Alexander Hamilton, shunned the former vice president. Retreating in a self-imposed exile, Burr left for Europe for a number of years. After traveling constantly to stand by her father during the trials, Theo now had to face her demons alone.

Tragedy struck in 1812 as Theo and Joseph moved to their summer home, "The Castle," on DeBordieu Beach to escape the oppressive heat of The Oaks. Their son, already sick with malaria, died a few weeks after the move. Burr, returning to New York to be closer to his daughter, convinced her to come after the holidays. The British were already making aggressive moves on the United States, and the waterways up the coast were known as dangerous; Joseph cautioned his wife against the trip, but gave in as he knew Theo wouldn't rest until she was once again with her father.

Writing her a letter of safe passage that would hopefully pass the British commander's inspection if the ship were boarded, Joseph stayed behind to deal with business matters as his wife went aboard the schooner *Patriot* on New Year's Eve 1812.

The trip north was to take five to six days. Comfortably situated in a cabin below deck, Theo stored away the trunks of clothing needed for the season of entertaining she would be again hostessing while in New York, and a portrait of herself to give to her father. On the second night, the *Patriot* met up with a British ship but was allowed safe passage due to the letter her husband had given her. After that, the ship's final fate is a mystery.

A storm was recorded as whipping the shoreline of Cape Hatteras, North Carolina, into a frenzy, and the *Patriot* may have been caught by the swells and sunk in the famous "Graveyard of the Atlantic." Many ships shared a similar destiny as they lay upon the rocks of the treacherous shore.

Another theory is that the ship was lured to wreck itself by the mooncussers—land pirates who tied a lantern around the neck of an animal and led the beast to walk the cliffs overlooking the water. Mistaking the glow to be that of a lighthouse or friendly port, ships during a storm would head straight toward their doom, only for the crew and passengers to be pillaged and murdered by the pirates. Indeed, a deathbed confession to an Alabama newspaperman in 1833 of a mooncusser, so named because they would shout at the moon for foiling their plans as it shone upon the water and warned away potential victims, said he and the others had killed everyone aboard the *Patriot* at Nags Head as the ship mistakenly trusted the false light. Fifteen years later, another pirate, "Old Frank" Burdick, told the same story of how he held the plank for a beautiful woman dressed in white as she stood unsteadily upon the board, pleading for the men to tell her husband and father of what had become of her. Burdick described how after the passengers' deaths, he and the pirates had plundered the ship and had seen the portrait of the same woman in the main cabin. In his book, *More Great Southern Mysteries*, R. Randall Floyd told of how the man had named one of the passengers as

Odessa Burr Alston and that she had chosen death over the prospect of sharing the pirate captain's bed.

But was that really the end of Theodosia? One story tells as the mooncussers swarmed the ship, the tenuous hold on her mind finally slipped away. The pirates bundled a woman and the portrait she refused to leave into a dingy and let her sail away into the night. Washing ashore onto the Outer Banks, the woman was taken in by a fisherman and his family and cared for, though no one was able to discover her name or why she'd held onto the portrait. As the years passed, her health began to fail. A doctor was called in to care for her at the fisherman's home, and her caretaker offered the portrait to the doctor as payment for his services. The legend states that the old woman rose from her bed in protest, claiming that the portrait was of herself and that she was on her way to New York to see her father. Tearing the painting from the wall, she ran to the sea and into the water, never to be seen again. The portrait washed up upon the sand the next day. The doctor retrieved it and returned with it to his home in Elizabeth City, North Carolina. Today, the portrait resides with a descendent of the Burr family who bought it from an art dealer after the doctor's family decided to part with it.

Theodosia's spirit is still searching the haunted stretch of land near Cape Hatteras lighthouse for her lost portrait. Her long white dress knotted in an invisible wind, she is still looking for her way home. Her ghost is also seen along the paths that cross her former home of The Oaks, along the strand near her summerhouse, and floating above the waves at Huntington Beach, South Carolina.

BLACK AGGIE

Hidden away in a tranquil courtyard behind the Dolley Madison House on the corner of H Street and Madison Place in Washington, DC, rests the foreboding life-sized, hooded monument of Black Aggie. Her story spans nearly a century, involving rumors of madness, loss of pregnancies, and possible death for those who chose to visit her at her former home in Pikeville, Maryland's Druid Ridge Cemetery.

Did Aggie's turmoil stem from its shady beginnings? The Adams Memorial, which is rumored to have been nicknamed "Grief" by Mark Twain in 1906, stood near the gravesite of Marion "Clover" Adams, the wife of a descendent of President John Quincy Adams. Having taken her own life in 1885, her husband enlisted the artist, Augustus Saint-Gaudens, to erect a reminder of his own deep loss in Washington's Rock Creek Cemetery. The artwork was surreal, its countenance serene yet heartbreaking. Resisting all demands for copies of the monument to be made available for the public, Adams mourned privately with the sculpture.

Years later, General Felix Agnus, Civil War veteran and publisher of the *Baltimore American* and *Baltimore Star* newspapers, commissioned sculptor Eduard L. A. Pausch for his own monument to be placed at the family plot. Unbeknownst to Agnus, Pausch copied the Adams Memorial to create the new bronze and told Agnus he was authorized to make such a duplicate. When the new statue was discovered, Saint-Gauden's widow was unable to convince Agnus to give up his monument and he was buried under its shadow in 1925.

The rumors of Black Aggie's wrath soon conjured stories of a both a witch and a wrongly executed nurse somehow buried beneath its feet. It was told her eyes would burn red as the clock struck the midnight hour and anyone who gazed upon her face would be instantly blinded. Any pregnant woman who crossed the shadow where no grass would grow would miscarry her child, and those foolish enough to sit on her lap on a moonless night would be crushed by her cold arms and dragged to hell. Charming.

The legend grew until crowds of visitors came to view the monument, fascinated by the story of a statue that exacted the revenge of a woman wronged. Local fraternities held part of their initiation rites at the monument, the pledges having to spend the night with their backs to the grave of General Agnus and dared to not turn around. One late night as a pledge laid at Aggie's feet, two fraternity brothers felt the air change between them as gray shadows clustered around the boy. As they began to warn the pledge, Black Aggie reportedly reached out to grab the boy, dragging him into her dark embrace. Scared, the fraternity brothers fled the scene when they encountered the cemetery night watchman. After hearing their story, the watchman went to the monument, only to find the body of a young man, dead from apparent fright.

Over the years, Black Aggie fell into disrepair. Not able to keep up with vandals and ne'er-do-wells, the statue became covered in graffiti and was left alone by the cemetery grounds people. In an effort to curtail further vandalism, the Agnus family donated the monument to the Smithsonian Institution in 1967, where it was lost in the shuffle of artifacts. Discovered again in the late 1980s, it was moved to its present resting place on the east side of Lafayette Square. No reports of further mischief have been reported.

GOLDEN GATE BRIDGE

Spanning the San Francisco Bay and built in 1937 to connect San Francisco to Marin County in California, the architectural wonder stretches 4,200 feet across the Golden Gate Strait and welcomes the waters of the Pacific Ocean. Painted a brilliant vermilion orange, the bridge is a favorite landmark of the coastal city and a beloved tourist destination. The bridge has a darker side, however, being the number one suicide spot in the world. With over thirteen hundred known deaths, the Golden Gate Bridge has been host to a jumper about every two weeks since its first suicide victim, Harold B. Wobler, who reportedly took a leisurely walk onto the suspension bridge, chatted with a tourist, and then leapt over the side ten weeks after the bridge's opening.

The Golden Gate Bridge. Courtesy of Stacey Graham.

With suicidal patrons favoring the view from the east side of the strait and looking at the famed city, the death toll rose as the disheartened chose a tragic path to the water and rocks below. Newspapers had kept a running tally of the suicides until that number neared one thousand. At that time, they chose to stop so as not to glamorize the deaths and to prevent anyone from claiming the notoriety of being the one thousandth body pulled from the cold waters of the bay. Today, the psychic residue of these victims may be felt and heard by visitors. On nights deep in the frequent fog of San Francisco, passersby can sometimes hear the screams of jumpers as the mist swallows them.

Bodies falling from the heights aren't the only things haunting this famed bridge. In 1853, the mighty USS *Tennessee* ran aground on the sharp rocks of the Golden Gate Strait. The current pulled the steamer ship quickly into the fog-shrouded waters, though luckily its 550 passengers and cargo of 14 chests of gold made it to land onto what is now named Tennessee Cove. Since the sinking, there have been reports of seeing the ship sail under the Golden Gate Bridge and into the fog. In one sighting, the crew of the USS *Kennison* told of the *Tennessee's* abandoned decks as it glided past the ship in November 1942 without even leaving a blip on its radar.

LONDON BRIDGE

The bridge built in 1831 and spanning London's River Thames really was falling down due to the stress of modern traffic. After city officials decided to put the bridge up for sale in 1962, American businessman and real estate developer Robert P. McCulloch bought the famous bridge and had it assembled stone by stone in Lake

Havasu, Arizona. With the pieces pre-coded for an easier assembly of this great puzzle, it took four years for forty workmen to piece the bridge together again in the desert, finally completing the project in October 1971.

A vintage postcard of the London Bridge in its original setting. Courtesy of the Library of Congress.

The Lord Mayor of London dedicated the grand re-opening of the bridge and the tourist attraction featured a variety of pubs and British-themed shops around the stone arches. During the ceremony, a woman saw four figures in old-fashioned British dress walking across the bridge. Assuming they were actors paid to give the bridge a little ambience, she thought nothing of it until they vanished before the eyes of her and others. With this believed to be a residual haunting, it's possible that the granite stone of the bridge held on to memories of the bridge's past. Granite has been thought to store energy, releasing it when conditions are favorable for a haunting.

After the bridge had been dismantled in London, ancient catacombs were found beneath the site. Identified as a plague pit used to bury victims, the vaults still contained human remains that may have attached themselves to the site where the former bridge stood for six hundred years and may have been built from the same materials used to build the bridge now standing in Arizona.

Other ghosts that walk the bridge to nowhere are a man and woman who stroll the bridge's expanse at night, and a woman dressed in black who paces the stones only to then stop and leap over the edge, disappearing into the water below.

GHOST TOWN: GARNET, MONTANA

One of my early experiences with the paranormal came from visiting a ghost town in the northwestern United States while on vacation. Now, you'd expect a ghost town to come with the prerequisite residual hauntings or at least a spooky outhouse. This town of Garnet, Montana, had its share of run-down buildings as it nestled in a wee valley in the mountains. A gold-mining town, it once held the riches of the mountain in its palm and miners flocked to pluck it from between the fingers of the hillside. It grew fat and rich for a time, but when the gold ran out, so did the miners, leaving behind a hotel, a general store, ramshackle houses, and large pockets dug into the nearby hills.

My family, along with other curious tourists, wandered through what was left of the town, trying to get a sense of what it was like in its heyday. Imagining dirty, desperate men returning from inside a mountain wasn't difficult; what remained of their cabins told the story better than any signage the Bureau of Land Management had provided. Ruined furniture, rusted pans left scattered around filthy cabins, and the feeling of failure permeated the broken walls of the houses. Why wouldn't there be a haunting? It seemed as if that was all there ever was here.

I entered the hotel slowly. Once there was grandeur of sorts; now it looked like a woman ruined by too many men and not enough self-respect. Plaster flaked from the walls and heavy tables stood in the middle of the first-floor dining room, looking strangely proud of weathering time and being able to show off their wounds left by drunken gunshots and the flying glass of old arguments. I followed my family upstairs to see the rooms, which had Plexiglas partitions so you could peer inside but not enter. In some rooms, the windows were left bare, sunshine squeaked in through the dirty glass and fell onto beds salvaged from the hotel and covered with old quilts. In others, the windows were covered and dusty light shone through the boards that swallowed the glass. These rooms held what seemed to be hundred-year-old garbage. It covered the floors and rose up the walls; it smelled like decay and made you want to turn away. Naturally, I couldn't.

As I got closer, my heart started to beat louder in my ears and my nose started to twitch. I felt lightheaded and wanted to run. I poked my head into the room and at once felt something rushing towards me. I am not particularly psychic—just enough to know when to get the heck out of a place. If I could describe it, I'd say it was pain, screaming, and confusion coming at me all at once. I backed away and my investigational gene kicked in. I checked out the other rooms to see if I experienced any similar occurrences and casually asked my husband if he had seen anything out of the ordinary. This man is as intuitive as a brick. "Nothing that a broom couldn't help," he replied.

I knew what I had felt had been unusual and I tested it again before we left the building. Again, my heart raced and my nose tingled, but this time there was no attack of emotion towards me. I could feel that it sat huddled in the corner, amidst the rubbish and filth, and watched as I moved out of sight and down the stairs, escaping into the light.

SIX

SPOOKY SEAS

From ill-fated pirates searching for their hidden treasure along the coast of Virginia to the shade of a woman caught in the strains of a long-faded melody while traveling on the *Queen Mary*, ships can be a hotbed of haunted activity. As sailors cross the seas, deaths happen: a fall from tall rigging onto the hard wooden deck, or the fury of a battle as sailors decide in an instant whether to brave the fight—or pay the consequences for their cowardice. Others are trapped in a memory: a late-night celebration is heard below deck while a madman steered the ship into the rocks leaving the *Lady Lovibond* to travel its phantom course for centuries.

Water has been associated with trapping paranormal phenomena. Could the ships be a floating portal to the otherworld?

RMS *QUEEN MARY*

Opulent, imposing, and crazy haunted, the RMS *Queen Mary* currently sits regally docked at the Port of Long Beach in California awaiting guests and a nightly crop of new ghost hunters. Built in Clydebank, Scotland, she began her long career crossing the Atlantic in 1936, ferrying the world's elite across the North Atlantic as the pride of the Cunard Line until World War II broke out in Europe in 1939. The ocean liner was then commissioned to carry troops, which nearly doubled her capacity from 2,410 passengers to 5,500 aboard the 1,000-foot ship. Nicknamed the "Gray Ghost" after her painted camouflaged transformation to blend into the ocean waves, the *Queen Mary* carried more than 800,000 troops by the end of the war. While avoiding contact with enemy vessels during the war, the *Queen Mary* did not escape tragedy. On October 2, 1942, the ship ran afoul of one of its escort cruisers, the HMS *Curacoa*. As it sliced through the smaller ship, 338 of the *Curacoa*'s sailors were left to drown, as it was against wartime policy to return for survivors. After the war, the ship was refurbished and returned to its swanky roots in July 1947.

By the early 1960s, the glamour once associated with crossing the ocean by ship had faded as airline travel became more affordable. The *Queen Mary*, with its lack of air conditioning and outdoor pools, was quickly becoming a relic. In 1967, she was sold to the city of Long Beach for use as a hotel and maritime museum. After over 1,000 transatlantic crossings, the luxury liner had finally come home.

Since its docking, hotel staff and visitors have reported multiple hauntings. Recognized as one of the most haunted objects in the world, there are an estimated 150 spirits roaming the Gray Ghost. Mysterious knocking upon the walls, disembodied voices, moving objects, and even the occasional appearance of a wet set of footprints on the deck of an empty pool add to the mystery of the grand old lady.

One unlucky ghost that is seen regularly is that of eighteen-year-old John Peddler. On July 10, 1966, the watertight Door 13 crushed Peddler during a training exercise in the propeller room in the part of the ship known as Shaft Alley. Because of the frequency in which people see the bearded young spirit wearing his blue coveralls in this location, he is known as the "Shaft Alley Spectre."

Fancy a swim? The *Queen Mary*'s famous pools are paranormal hotspots for the pulse-challenged set. The first-class swimming pool, closed off for decades, has reports of ladies dressed in 1930s-era swimsuits cavorting around the now-empty pool, as well as a woman dressed in a miniskirt. Other activity includes seeing a pair of wet footprints pad off to dressing room from the deck and hearing phantom splashing from the pool. In the second-class pool area, the shade of Jackie, a small girl who drowned, has often been heard and felt by guests. Jackie has also been seen in other areas of the ship.

The ghost of Senior Second Officer W. E. Stark has been found wandering the deck as well as his old sleeping quarters. In September 1949, Stark drank from an old gin bottle containing tetrachloride and lime juice, not realizing the bottle had been repurposed to hold the cleaning fluid. Falling into a coma, the officer died three days later only to return in spectral form.

Deep within the ship's hull, near the bosun's locker, investigators have recorded odd pounding noises. This was the area that crashed into the *Curacoa*—is that area of the ship caught in a residual haunting of that fateful day?

One of the more horrifying stories surrounding the great ship is of its days as a troop transport. While men readied themselves for war, their thoughts turned to their stomachs. The cook's fare was reportedly so terrible that the men rioted, stuffing the cook into the oven where he burned to death. His final screams have been heard in the kitchen area.

If staying at the hotel and wanting a little paranormal activity, request to stay near cabin B340. Legend has it that the ghost of a purser can't cross over and makes an uproar. Faucets turning on by themselves and bedsheets being tossed across the room, as well as other unexplained phenomena, have forced the hotel to no longer rent this room to their guests.

A woman has been seen gently swaying to the music of a long-dead melody in the area known as the Queens Salon, once the first-class lounge. Dressed in a flowing white gown, she's thought to be attached to a particular piano, occasionally gliding into a waltz within the shadows of the room. Could it be one of the stars who traveled across the Atlantic in the ocean liner's heyday? Celebrities such as Elizabeth Taylor, Mary Pickford, and Greta Garbo once sailed in style, as well as dignitaries such as Winston Churchill and the Duke and Duchess of Windsor, as the *Queen Mary* cut through the rough waves of the Atlantic. My question is, who is the Lady in White waiting for?

As more reports of paranormal activity come in for this amazing vessel, the Queen Mary Hotel has embraced its ghostly reputation and offers spirit tours and investigations aboard the ship. Be sure to ask for a room with a boo.

The USS *Constellation*. Courtesy of the Library of Congress.

USS *CONSTELLATION*

A whiff of gunpowder going past the sharp nose of a naval officer in 1955 helped cement the legends of the haunting of the USS *Constellation*, docked in Baltimore, Maryland's Inner Harbor. The officer had been taking a photograph aboard the old ship near midnight for a story in the *Baltimore Sun*, when the scent of past battles wafted through the open harbor. When the story ran with the man's accompanying photograph of a blurry figure dressed in his naval uniform marching across the top deck, the *Constellation*'s ghostly history began to unfold and the mystery of how the incarnation of two ships named *Constellation* would become the resting place of multiple ghosts.

Built in Maryland in 1797, the first ship to hold the name was built as a thirty-six-gun frigate. Along with its sister ships, the USS *Constitution* and the USS *United States*, their mission was to protect the new nation's ships from attacks from pirates roaming the waters from their shores of North Africa and the Caribbean. The *Constellation*'s designer, David Stodder, gave the ship sharp bowlines, making it cut across the waves faster than the rest and earning the nickname "Yankee Race Horse." Her captain Thomas Truxtun, a veteran of the Revolutionary War with strong views on discipline, ran his crew with an efficient and strict hand in order to keep them all alive.

A month after entering the dangerous waters near the island of Nevis in the West Indies, the *Constellation* entered into battle with the French ship *L'Insurgente* in 1799. Reducing the French ship to scattered timbers, the *Constellation* was on its way to becoming one of America's foremost fighting machines. However, during the battle, one of the sailors failed at his station. Either falling asleep or, more likely, leaving his post, Neil Harvey was found guilty of being a coward and thus a traitor during the clash. Truxtun had no mercy for the man, ordering Harvey to be tied to the business end of a cannon and blown apart by the forthcoming explosion of the ball ripping through his body. Psychic Sybil Leek visited the ship with Hans Holzer years later. Describing the man in Holzer's book, *Ghosts: True Encounters with the World Beyond*, Leek said he was unable to materialize because "he was in bits and pieces and thus remembered 'himself' in this gruesome fashion."

The vessel went on to sail around the world, guarding ships off the coast of South America and visiting ports in Hawaii and China before docking in Norfolk, Virginia.

The second *Constellation* was rebuilt as a sloop in 1853, using many of the old timbers of the previous frigate. It returned to active service in 1859 as the rumbling of the Civil War began; its job was to now intercept slave ships on their way to the southern coast of the United States. After its duty finished during the war, the ship returned to dock and began the slow process of rot. Towed to Baltimore Harbor in the mid-1950s after a concerned citizen's group raised money to save the old ship, the *Constellation* sat waiting for repairs. That's when stories of ghosts creeping along the decks of the abandoned ship began to circulate.

Was the scent of gunpowder the naval officer smelled a reminder of old wounds the *Constellation* had endured a hundred years before? The photograph in the paper showed a man reaching across his waist as if to draw a sword against an unwelcome intruder upon the deck of his ship. The figure may have been wearing gold epaulets, a sign of his captain's rank. Could it have been Captain Truxtun defending his ship once more from pirates? In 1964, a Catholic priest was touring the *Constellation*. After he finished exploring the ship, he complimented the staff on his guide—a man dressed in a late-eighteenth-century naval uniform who had shown him the inner workings of the great ship. The staff admitted there were no costumed guides aboard the *Constellation* at that time.

Truxtun has been reported as being seen on the ship accompanied by the smell of gunpowder along with others. Visitors have described feelings of energy whirling around them, as if they were caught within the fury of a battle, men rushing to their stations and preparing for the worst. This psychic imprint of fear and excitement may have resulted in staining the wooden decks of one of the oldest ships in the United States Navy with a residual haunting. Perhaps the result of those battles culminated in the deaths of two crew members. The often-sighted hauntings depict one who hanged himself and is now seen on the gun and forecastle decks, and the other crew member running for his life on the top deck.

Other reports of a small boy have circulated around the mystery of the ship. It was common to have boys onboard as assistants, either running powder to the sailors to load the guns or as surgical assistants to the ship's doctor. Sylvia Leek felt the presence of child who had been murdered by two sailors, either by accident or design; his spirit wanders the ship in search of a way home.

A more recently departed soul is said to return to the historic ship. A watchman named Carl Hansen roamed the vessel for years during the mid-twentieth century until losing his job to an alarm system. His spirit is said to pop in on the lower decks to play a hand of cards, and once was seen sitting next to a young girl during a Halloween party.

The USS *Constellation* is open to the public at Baltimore's Inner Harbor at Pier 1.

THE *FLYING DUTCHMAN:* HARBINGER OF DOOM

Note to self: when faced with the choice of being sassy with the Devil and doomed to sail the wicked seas for all eternity or quietly round the Cape of Good Hope in South Africa—pick the latter. The legend of the *Flying Dutchman* has as many tendrils as the kraken, each with its own dire warnings of death and destruction for those who are foolish enough to wait out the haunted ship's return during a storm.

The name *Flying Dutchman* refers to the ship's captain. In the Dutch version, the seventeenth-century skipper was named van Straaten, though he is better known in maritime lore as Hendrick Van der Decken. As bad weather threatened to swallow the cape on one of their journeys, his men begged him to steer the ship to safe waters or put into port. As he screamed to the heavens that he would not be cheated of his chance to round the famously dangerous point of South Africa, the crew mutinied. In a rage, Van der Decken killed the mutineers' leader and threw his body overboard as the clouds approached and their death edged closer. As the sailor's corpse hit the water, the wind stilled and the storm ceased its advance. Shadows swirled upon the deck, twisting into the shape of a man until the Devil was standing in front of the captain. His mind addled with pride and drunk on power, Van der Decken fired his pistol at the being. The Devil hates that. He doomed the captain and his crew to sail the oceans until Judgment Day, bringing death to all who spied them across the water. To make it especially uncomfortable, the Devil added that gall should be their drink and their meat would be red-hot iron. I think he was just being petty.

In other tales, the haunted ship's captain played a regular game of dice with the Devil, much like the Scottish legend of Glamis Castle's hidden room, where the pair played for the lord's soul. In this case, Van der Decken lost, and he and his shipmates were bound to sail with no port to take them in—there was no rest for the wicked. Another version of the *Flying Dutchman* story tells of how the ship would approach vessels under the pretext of exchanging letters to be taken to the next port. If the letters were opened and read, however, the ship would meet with a cruel end.

One adaptation of the tale gave the captain a second chance at redemption. Every seven years the ship could put into port, giving Van der Decken time to find a woman to love him unconditionally, but since the ship is still sailing, I suppose the whole "crew of dead men" thing may be a deal breaker.

As the *Flying Dutchman* glided into salty folklore, sightings of the ship became harbingers of disaster for those unlucky enough to catch a glimpse of her misty sails. Stories of sailors who ran afoul of the *Dutchman* told of illness sweeping through the ranks, resulting in some deaths and feeding the notoriety of the legend. Spying the deadman's crew on the deck of the rotting ship was sometimes seen as a warning to take heed of their position as a storm would soon overtake them—many ships turned back to safe harbor instead of risking the challenge of the phantom vessel. Along the Cape of Good Hope, there have been reported sightings of the ship since the seventeenth century. When one British ship returned home from its travels in 1835, the crew told of how the *Dutchman* came so close that they were afraid the two ships would collide—then it mysteriously vanished.

The British ship HMS *Bacchante*, in 1881, rounded the tip of the African continent only to watch the *Flying Dutchman* appear before it. The ship's lookout strained to see against dark waters the early morning of July 11. One of the men on the *Bacchante* recorded in his notes that they had seen the ship being bathed in a red light, but when the sailors rushed to the forecastle to get a better look, there was no sign of the mighty ship ever existing. Thirteen people saw her at 4 a.m., and at 10:45 a.m. the seaman who had first alerted the crew fell from the topmast and was "smashed to atoms." One of the midshipmen on the voyage was the future King George V of Great Britain, who escaped the curse but never forgot his brush with the hopeless ship.

Numerous reports of seeing the *Flying Dutchman* have continued into the twentieth century. In the spring of 1939, dozens of beachgoers reported seeing the ship off the coast of South Africa. Though it was assumed most of these people were not familiar with the rigging of a three-hundred-year-old merchant ship, their detailed accounts of what the ship looked like before it faded in front of their eyes brought new life to the story of the old ship. The *Flying Dutchman* faded from sight at last in 1941 with the last reported account of the ship sailing off the coast of Cape Town, gliding into Table Bay, and vanishing.

THE *STAR OF INDIA*

The siren song of the wide-open sea can lure the bravest of men to their deaths. The freedom they sought away from the constraints of land can be a strong pull with the promise of adventure and a steady job on the crew of a tall ship. The *Euterpe*, later known as the *Star of India*, began her tale in 1863 at the shipyards at Ramsey on the Isle of Man. One of the first ships made of iron, she glided through the water as a cargo vessel working the Indian jute route.

Her first voyage had a bit of a rocky start. In 1864, a Spanish brig hit the *Euterpe* during the night, resulting in the jib boom being damaged. The crew refused to sail with the ship in desperate need of repair and mutinied, demanding that they put in to Anglesey, an island off the northwest coast of Wales. There, the men were arrested for their actions and forced into hard labor. Did they curse the ship on her subsequent travels as they being were taken away? Later, a cyclone off Madras forced Captain Storry to cut away her masts, and they slowly made their way back to Trincomalee, near Sri Lanka, and Calcutta for more repairs. As they made their way back to England, her captain died and was buried at sea.

Sold in 1871 to the Shaw Savill Line of London, the *Euterpe* brought a different cargo west. Emigrants braved the cold Atlantic winds, crossing into New Zealand, Australia, California, and Chile. After twenty-one successful round-the-world trips, the ship was then sold to many new owners until 1906, when it was renamed the *Star of India* by the Alaska Packers' Association of San Francisco. By 1923, the ship was no longer in active service, being replaced by the faster and more efficient steamer ships of the day. The *Star of India* was towed to San Diego in 1926. A restoration was planned to refurbish the ship and make it the centerpiece of the Zoological Society of San Diego's upcoming museum and aquarium. Unfortunately, the ensuing Great Depression and World War II halted all plans and the ship was left in its berth to rot.

Thirty years passed before author and captain Alan Villiers rescued the great ship by inspiring citizens to form the Star of India Auxiliary in 1959 and began raising money to restore the ship. By 1976, the ship was seaworthy again. Now housed at the Maritime Museum of San Diego, it sails once a year and is open for tours.

So what walks the decks during the quiet Southern Californian nights? As the fourth-oldest ship to survive in the United States, she has tales to tell. In 1884, a teenaged stowaway, John Campbell, was discovered on board the *Euterpe* and put to work for his passage. While scurrying about the masts, he lost his footing and fell to the decks one hundred feet below the towering sails, breaking both of his legs. His shipmates carried him to his bunk, where he died three days later. Now, as a warning to stay clear of the mast, visitors have reported feeling a cold hand pass over their skin.

Toward the bow of the ship lay the anchor-chain locker. Years ago, as the crew began to raise the heavy anchor and set out into open water, they didn't notice a crew member missing. He had been working in the locker and was crushed as the chain filled the dark storage space, his screams muffled under the noise of the machinery. Today, a cold spot lingers in this compartment.

Though no one has fired up the stove for years, reports have been made of the smell of freshly baked bread greeting visitors in the galley and dining room areas. Pots and pans lining the galley walls have been known to move on their own even as the ship itself sits in calm waters. Perhaps even spectral sailors get hungry.

LADY LOVIBOND

Was it superstition that doomed the tall ship *Lady Lovibond* or simply the jealous rage of a brokenhearted sailor? According to sea lore, a woman on board a ship caused nothing but misery. Fearing their presence would inflame the passions of the men who had been out on the water for far too long and distract sailors from their duties, most captains banished women from the deck before they set off for open water. Setting sail on a Friday also tempted fate, as it was believed that this was the day Christ was crucified. Coupled with the fear of the number thirteen, Friday the 13th of February in 1748 became the triple whammy of bad luck before the *Lady Lovibond* even left harbor.

Bound for Oporto, Portugal, with a heavy cargo of flour, wine, meat, and gold, the captain, Simon Peel (also recorded as Simon Reed), boarded the ship with his bride, Annetta, and the wedding party to accompany him on the voyage. Sailing down the River Thames to cross the English Channel on a clear winter's night, there was nothing but the sound of celebrating below deck to carry across the dark water.

Before them lay the Goodwin Sands, off of Kent County, near Deal in southwestern England. Stretching ten-miles long and believed to have once been a small island named Lomea, which was lost to the sea, the quicksand had claimed nearly two thousands ships and countless lives. Immortalized in William Shakespeare's *The Merchant of Venice*, the sandbank had a reputation that preceded it:

> *The Goodwins, I think they call the place; a very dangerous flat and fatal, where the carcasses of many a tall ship lie buried, as they say…*

As the wedding party feasted in the warmth of the Captain's quarters that night, a sailor roamed the deck above. The ship's first mate, John Rivers, had once courted Annetta and her betrayal at marrying the captain drove him insane. That night, he pulled a blunt clublike belaying pin from the rail and approached the seaman steering the ship from behind. Bludgeoning the man, Rivers took control of the ship's wheel, steering it toward the dangerous Goodwin Sands. As the ship ran aground, all aboard were lost, the victims of a madman's rage.

Questions swelled around the testimony of River's mother at the inquiry. Had she known of his intentions? She testified that she had heard him vow revenge, but the court could not prove his plot as the disaster had happened so close to a known hazard. After the wreck was ruled a "misadventure," the *Lady Lovibond*'s tragedy faded into whispers at local pubs.

Fifty years had passed since the ship sank beneath the waves, but on February 13, 1798, Captain James Westlake of the *Edenbridge* reported sighting the haunted vessel. As it approached his ship, he avoided a collision only by turning the wheel quickly, his ears catching for a moment the sound of a party below the deck as the ship sailed by. A fishing boat also reported seeing the *Lady Lovibond* in its final moments that night. The crew watched as the ship ran aground the Goodwin Sands, splintering in the wind and water. Sending out lifeboats to rescue the survivors, they were met with only silence.

The *Lady Lovibond* appeared once again on the one-hundredth anniversary of its destruction. To villagers on the shore at Deal, it appeared so real that they too sent out boats to rescue those who lived. As the men approached the ship, however, it faded from sight. The last reported sighting of the doomed ship was in 1948. Captain Bull Prestwick told authorities that the vessel looked real, but glowed a mysterious green. There were no official sightings of the *Lady Lovibond* in 1998, though I have my fingers crossed for a midnight showing in 2048.

THE GHOST SHIP OF THE HAUNTED WOODS

Some areas are just ripe for a haunting. Off the dark waters of the Chesapeake Bay in Mathews County, near Gloucester, Virginia, bands of pirates searching for their lost treasure scour the woodlands in an area known as the Old House Woods or the Haunted Woods. Named for an old abandoned cottage that had once caught fire then put itself out, then again caught fire years later and burned to the ground, the heavily forested fifty-acre plot of land hosts the appearance of two phantom ships above the treetops.

Busy seaports dotted the region during the period between pre–Revolutionary War America and the Civil War, becoming thick with privateers and those willing to take your goods off your hands with or without your permission. Carrying chests of presumably ill-gotten loot, one band of unlucky pirates buried the booty on the banks of Whites Creek adjacent to the Old House Woods and left to pillage more villages only to be drowned at sea. One skeleton-faced phantom in particular rises from the water dressed as a pirate, ascending over the trees and into the woods. In the late nineteenth century, one man described that while fishing at the mouth of Whites Creek, he viewed the ghostly ship sail up the creek and onto the beach—and into the woods as it floated above the ground. Is it the same ship that eyewitnesses have seen for two hundred years hovering over the trees and Whites Creek?

A long-lost Spanish galleon also haunts the creek. Reported with the sails either billowing in an absent wind or tied tight to their masts, the ship has been seen soundlessly floating above witnesses as they look up. If you visit the banks of Whites Creek, it's said you can face the woods and see where the ship leaves a groove in the tree line where it docks before the crew jumps to the ground. The forest seems to light with an unearthly green glow as the pirates search the area looking for that last bit of treasure. Locals have heard the sounds of digging and shovels striking rock. Legend tells that once the light flashes three times, it's your sign to leave the pirates to their work; otherwise you'll be chased off by two headless black dogs. I wouldn't take my chances.

The Battle of Worcester in 1651 left Britain's King Charles II scrambling to secure part of his fortune in case he needed to flee or else end up as his father, Charles I—headless. After he sent a crew to nearby Jamestown with the treasure, the ship went up the wrong waterway due to stormy weather and found itself at Whites Creek. Stranded upriver and thinking that they'd be sitting ducks for marauders the captain decided the area would be safe for the time being and ordered his men to unload the chests and hide the treasure on shore with the intent of retrieving it and making the passage to Jamestown under safer conditions. However, the captain's judgment in safe spots was apparently as poor as his steering skills, as they were attacked and robbed as they dug. After finishing off the crew, the thieves carried the chests deeper into the forest, burying part of the naval crew with them and planned to return later; however, they were soon captured by local authorities and put to death—leaving the location of the treasure hidden forever. Those close to this paranormally active area swear they've heard and seen the thieves searching the woods, shovels and lanterns in hand, searching for what they think they stole fair and square.

SEVEN

BETWIXT AND BETWEEN IN HAUNTED HOTELS

Can a hotel itself be haunted? Ask anyone who has ever lived in a haunted house. As our energy passes through the hallways and rented rooms, we leave a trace of ourselves that binds us to the places we touch and what memories we leave.

Hotels are a microcosm of humanity: joy, grief, heartbreak, and romance can influence an object's vibration and leave the remnants of a brief—but poignant—visit. The stories of these hotels only scratch the surface of the drama that continually evolves as guests check in but never check out. As a haunted object, hotels become one of the larger items on our list of spooky stuff, leaving us to ask if that lingering odor of cigarette smoke in our room wasn't just a coincidence. Weary visitors may leave an impression of more than a dented pillow.

THE CRESCENT HOTEL

Sometimes the most beautiful façade can mask even the most nefarious deeds. The Victorian-era Crescent Hotel overlooking the resort town of Eureka Springs, Arkansas, stands proudly on the crest of the West Mountain, its history wrapped in the misplaced trust of others.

The Crescent Hotel in Eureka Springs, Arkansas. Courtesy of Beth Bartlett.

In a time when many were looking for fast and effective cures to their ailments, people flocked to Eureka Springs, famous for its "healing waters." To handle the influx of visitors, the Eureka Springs Improvement Company began construction on the hotel in 1884. Designed for luxury, the hotel boasted a magnificent dining room that at one time seated over five hundred people, numerous towers, and more importantly—indoor plumbing. The hotel opened two years later and quickly filled to cater to those with delicate health and large wallets. By the turn of the century, however, people realized the healing waters weren't as effective as other treatments, and the craze slowly died down—taking the Crescent with it.

After a brief period as the Crescent College and Conservatory for Young Women, the hotel was sold to a man of dubious character: Norman Baker. Reopening the hotel as a cancer center and health resort, Baker promised his guests that they would return from their treatments cancer-free. Unfortunately, his "cure" was a scam. Baker would later be convicted of fraud for selling his miracle elixirs to hopeful patients through the mail. Sent to Leavenworth Prison to serve a four-year sentence, the investigation showed he had bilked cancer sufferers out of nearly $4 million. While not directly contributing to the deaths of his guests with his version of the "healing waters," he was found to have hastened their painful demise by delaying other treatments.

The Crescent Hotel changed hands multiple times throughout the rest of the nineteenth century, with each owner attempting to restore the building to its former glory. In 1997, Marty and Elise Roenigk purchased the property and set out to restore the "Grand Lady of the Ozarks." Five years later, the hotel was thriving, in part due to the care of its staff—and its ghosts.

Many of the stories told by visitors revolve around a spirit they believe was an Irish stonemason who had worked on the original building. While on the roof, he lost his footing and fell to his death where room 218 now stands. Fond of teasing the living, Michael is often blamed for playing tricks on visitors by flipping the lights on and off, slamming doors, and pounding on the walls.

Housekeeping supervisor Nancy Reynolds remembers her early days as a housekeeper: "I'd hear my name called all the time. It would be faint, like someone at the other end of the hall. Other housekeepers still have that happen, too. Also doors slamming, hearing stuff behind you; it's weird." When asked how many entities she thinks may be roaming the halls, she replied, "More than anyone knows, I'm sure. The only time I've seen anything, I didn't know who it was. It was solid enough that I thought one of my housekeepers was behind me, but when I turned, there was no one there—no one down the hall either. I don't know who it was, though. What disturbed me more was that I was undisturbed by it." Could she have seen one of the Crescent's other famous residents? The former cancer patient, Theodora? Reputedly seen in room 419 by the staff, Theodora introduces herself, then vanishes.

Are the ghosts keeping an eye on the Crystal Dining Room chandeliers? Reynolds has received notes containing prisms from the elegant fixtures from guests who believed they brought a ghost home along with their ill-gotten souvenir. The dining room also has reports of dancers dressed in their late-nineteenth-century finery whirling around the room when the rest of the world is asleep.

There are not only human ghosts walking the grounds. Lead cook Sandi Rowe remembers meeting up with Rufus after his unfortunate tangle with an automobile: "We once had a hotel cat named Rufus. He always met me every morning just past the gift shop as I came in for work. He was hit by a car [and killed] on the Friday before Memorial Day weekend; I remember the time and date because it was so shocking. Five or six months later, I went in to work and saw him coming to meet me past the gift shop. He was walking toward me, and he lifted a paw, and disappeared."

Other apparitions in what is called "America's Most Haunted Hotel" have been sighted. A young woman who had stayed at the Crescent during its time as a women's college jumped from a balcony and guests at the hotel have reported hearing her screams mimicking her final descent. Dubious owner Baker has also been spotted in the old recreation room in the basement while wearing his signature lavender shirt and white linen suit.

People report that if you purchase a snow globe at the Crescent Hotel and place it in the sun, the water will mysteriously turn red. Courtesy of LaMishia Allen Photography.

The Crescent Hotel welcomes paranormal investigators and the curious to find out for themselves about the haunting of the grand hotel with nightly tours. If you do stay, please tell Theodora hello—she's dying to meet you.

DON CESAR BEACH HOTEL

Perched on the soft white sand of St. Pete Beach outside of Tampa, Florida, sits a brilliant pink bijou of a hotel overlooking the turquoise water of the gulf. The Mediterranean-style building played host to presidents, authors, and infamous celebrities such as Al Capone since its opening in 1928, but its partylike atmosphere features a love story that replays itself while the living look on.

While touring Europe as a young man, the future owner of the Don CeSar, Thomas Rowe, attended the opera *Maritana* in London and fell in love with the lead, Lucinda. After her performances each night, they met a fountain near the Royal Opera House, and as their love deepened, they made plans to elope after her final concert. As the day neared, Rowe readied for his new life with the dark-haired Spanish beauty. Learning of their daughter's plans, however, Lucinda's parents disapproved of the match and forced her to return with them to Spain. The lovers were to never meet again. His heart shattered, Rowe returned to the United States. His letters to Lucinda were returned unaccepted and unopened by her parents until word came that his love had passed away, the victim of a sudden illness. Never forgetting the love of her youth, Lucinda's parents wrote that she had one final message for Rowe from her deathbed: "Time is infinite. I wait for you by our fountain...to share our timeless love, our destiny is time."

Years later, Rowe would name the hotel after the hero of the *Maritana*, the opera where he had met Lucinda so long before. Rowe's love for the woman he'd lost manifested in the hotel, which became one of the grandest in the region. He also commissioned a fountain similar to the one where he and Lucinda had their clandestine meetings. Set in the lobby on the ground floor, the fountain reportedly fashioned a large winged angel pouring water from a vase into the swan-encircled pond: a perfect setting for a lover's tryst.

Rowe died in the hotel on May 5, 1940, but never quite left the building. His white-suited ghost has been seen roaming the fifth-floor hallways or smiling in greeting as guests check in to his self-proclaimed Pink Castle before he fades into the Florida sunshine as it filters through the grand windows. After his passing, the hotel was left to his estranged wife, who had neither the inclination nor good business sense to keep the hotel running at its former speed. When she eventually lost the property to the United States government during World War II, the hotel rotated through various uses: an Army hospital, a convalescent center, and a veteran's administrative office until the once-lovely hotel became a shell of a building, its previous glory lost to a different age.

It was during this time that the fountain was removed, being thought to have gotten in the way of those trying to navigate the lobby, and the hotel fell into further disrepair. Changing hands, the hotel was bought in 1972 by businessman William Bowman Jr., who restored the hotel and reinstated another fountain in the former fountain's place. During construction, a note was found under the lobby floor, left by a previous superintendent who apologized for demolishing the famous fountain under direction of the owners and removing the "spot of beauty" forever. There have since been successive fountains in the lobby, but none have had the charm nor staying power of Rowe's token of affection to his first love. After renovations to the hotel in 1987, Rowe's spirit would often be seen with a raven-haired ghostly woman who accompanied the phantom as he roamed the corridors and in the courtyard. It seems Lucinda kept her promise to be with him for eternity.

The hotel is now owned by the Loews Hotel chain and has been restored once again at its majestic spot overlooking the warm sands of the gulf and, perhaps, a pair of long-lost lovers.

WHITE EAGLE SALOON

Across the river from Portland, Oregon's shanghai tunnels, the White Eagle Saloon welcomed the seedier side of frontier life in the early nineteenth century. After the work whistle blew, the men left the docks hungry and searching for more than food. They'd board the trolley that lumbered up Mississippi Avenue and leapt off in droves as the conductor yelled out "Next stop, Bucket of Blood!" So named for the brawls that erupted in the saloon and crept out into the night, the White Eagle's less-than-pristine reputation rivaled the notorious tunnels in Portland's Chinatown.

The two-storied brick building housed a "white" brothel upstairs and a "black and Chinese" brothel in the basement. The lonely spirit of Rose wanders the thirteen rooms upstairs, her weeping now heard to echo in the empty rooms. Rose was a working girl and considered the personal property of the saloon manager. One of her paying customers had fallen in love with the girl and wanted to take her away from this life of danger and dead-ends. Frightened by the prospect of confronting the manager, Rose refused. When her young lover faced his cruel adversary, he was nearly beaten to death. Undaunted and sure of his love, he again pleaded with Rose to run away with him. When she refused, he grew enraged and stabbed her to death in one of the upstairs bedrooms. But Rose didn't let that little mishap daunt her spirit—recent patrons have reported being propositioned by a woman who may be the ghost of the long-dead prostitute.

Before the saloon was owned by the McMenamin Corporation, the previous owner had ventured upstairs only when needed. The rooms all have working locks, though each time he attempted to enter the rooms, some would refuse to open while others stood ready for visitors. He closed off the upper level and simply let the inhabitants be.

Another spirit that haunts the upstairs is that of Sam. Taken in as a child, he worked in the saloon for most of his life. When he died an old man, his shade continued to watch over his home. His belongings remained in his room, though they have been found moved to other rooms on the second floor. Passersby have reported seeing the image of a man gazing from the second-floor windows as they walk by. Perhaps he's watching over them too.

The basement held the secrets of the saloon. The black and Chinese women brought in from the docks or sold as virtual slaves were held in tiny rooms and made to sell their bodies in lieu of beatings from the management. Children born to the women were rumored to have been disposed of quickly, so the women could return to work. The spirits of these desperate women clog the atmosphere; their pain is etched into the walls and marks the air. One manager of the saloon in recent times had an office in the basement.

At night, over the low hum of his television, he would hear music cascading down from the bar after closing. Another time, coins fell from the ceiling onto the floor. Once, he felt what appeared to be a strong earthquake that shook the building to its core. When turning to the television, he could find no reports for what he had just felt. A waitress, beginning her descent down into the basement, was shoved from behind, in full view of the owner. She tumbled the length of the stairs and sustained minor injuries.

The spirits apparently have frequented the bathrooms. One lady, while using the facilities, entered into a toilet paper fight over the stall walls with a friend, only to discover there was no one there, her friend had left much earlier.

Rooms are now available for rental on the upper floor. Are you willing to brave the night and share a room with Sam and Rose?

DRISKILL HOTEL AND THE SUICIDE BRIDES

Everything is bigger in Texas: cars, hair…and ghost stories. Built in the late nineteenth century, the Driskill Hotel in Austin, Texas, is no exception, taking pride in its unique guests and even including a fact sheet of the resident ghosts you may encounter when staying at the hotel. Cattle baron Colonel Jesse Driskill opened the hotel in 1886 after making his fortune selling beef to the Confederate Army during the Civil War. Wanting his hotel to be the finest in Austin, he spent nearly $8,000 on the corner lot of 6th Street and Brazos and started construction on hotel that cost a total of $400,000 to complete. This time, the Texan went a little too big. The cost of staying at the luxury hotel was too much for most people and the Driskill fell on hard times. Reportedly losing the hotel in a card game to his brother-in-law a few years later, Jesse Driskill died penniless, still clinging to the dream of his once-grand hotel.

Successive owners breathed new life into the hotel, adding 129 rooms to the original 60 rooms plus a 30-foot tower by 1930, and watched it become the center of the Austin social scene in the twentieth century. Society weddings, inaugural balls, and even the famous first date of future president Lyndon B. Johnson and Claudia Taylor (better known as Lady Bird Johnson)took place in the Driskill's ballroom. The Johnsons often returned to the hotel, using it as campaign headquarters during his congressional career and staying there during presidential visits.

While the hotel's fame and beauty waxed and waned through the years, a darker side of the property began to earn its own notoriety. Samantha Houston, the four-year-old daughter of a Texan senator who stayed at the Driskill while the senate was in session, tragically died after falling down the grand staircase in 1887. Within a week, her ghost was reported bouncing a ball in the first-floor lobby as well as being seen and heard giggling near the second-floor ladies room and the stairs leading to the mezzanine. Samantha's father had a painting commissioned of the young girl shortly after her death that now hangs on the fifth floor of the hotel. Marketing manager Laura Pettitt said in an interview with KVUE News in October 2012: "People say once in a while you can catch her giving a smile, and her expression will change in the painting." Samantha loves a little extra attention and rattles the doors of the Yellow Rose Suite near the painting when she's feeling mischievous.

Colonel Driskill wasn't about to give up his hotel without a fight from the afterlife. His ghost has been reported smoking the cigars he loved in life and turning lights off and on while visiting guests in their rooms. A ladies' man, his ghost has been blamed for a disembodied head appearing during a shower of the lead singer of the alternative rock band Concrete Blonde, Johnette Napolitano, while another time helping Eurythmics singer Annie Lennox choose a dress for a performance. Laying out two outfits on the bed before taking a shower, Lennox returned to find only one on the bed, while the other had been hung up in the closet.

The Maximilian Room at the Driskill Hotel has a set of mirrors commissioned by the Mexican Emperor Maximilian as a gift to his European bride, Carlotta. After her death in 1927, the large gilded-framed mirrors were boxed up at their home and put into storage in New Orleans, Louisiana. When they were discovered a few years later, the Driskill Hotel bought the mirrors and installed them in the room that was used as a gentleman's smoking area. Visitors have reported seeing the figure of a woman staring back at them while they gaze in the mirrors, but when they turn around, no one was there.

Brides haven't always been lucky at the Driskill. While many begin their new lives in a sea of well-wishers and happiness, two of the now-famous women of the Driskill live on, trapped in a haunting and known as the Suicide Brides.

One of the more paranormally active ghosts at the hotel is Suicide Bride No. 1. In 1969, the night before her wedding, the groom called off the ceremony. After hanging herself in the bathroom of room 427, her ghost is occasionally seen walking down the fourth-floor hallways wearing a wedding gown. Most often observed by guests staying at the hotel for a wedding or bachelorette party, the ghost is considered good luck if the bride sees her before the nuptials.

Suicide Bride No. 2 is most often referred to as the "Houston Bride." Twenty years after the death of Suicide Bride No. 1, a woman from Houston checked in to room 427 after being jilted by her fiancé. After visiting the luxurious room, she left to melt the numbers off his credit card by spending $10,000 on an extravagant shopping spree. Weighed down with packages, the woman returned to her room around 1 a.m. and extracted her most important—and lethal—purchase: a pistol. In the same bathroom where a bride had taken her own life twenty years before, the Houston Bride laid down in the bathtub with a pillow and her new firearm. Discharging the pistol through the pillow so as not to make a sound, the woman died alone in the hotel bathtub, her blood filling the porcelain vessel.

Ten years later, two women staying at the hotel decided to take a late-night visit around the haunted property. The fourth floor was under reconstruction to update the rooms, so it was not well traveled by guests. At 1 a.m., they saw a woman walk past them, her arms filled with purchases, and stand in front of room 427 while struggling with her room key. Asking the woman if she was bothered by all of the construction noise, the woman responded coldly, saying, "No, I don't mind at all" and then entered the room.

The next morning, the women asked the manager about the guest staying in the closed-off area of the hotel. Telling the ladies that no one was checked in to that section of rooms, he showed them room 427, which had neither a bed nor a toilet. No guest would have been in that room that needed working plumbing for long. There were stories, however, that the hotel has had problems refurbishing that particular room. The walls had to be repainted four times as the paint peeled from the walls, and the bathtub—though there was no running water in the bathroom at the time—would fill up with translucent water, yet the tub hadn't been used in many years.

A SLIVER OF HAUNTING: THE BORDEN HOUSE

Lizzie Borden took an axe
Gave her mother forty whacks;
When she saw what she had done
Gave her father forty-one

Sèphera Girón knows the rhyme associated with the Borden House well. Visiting the bed-and-breakfast in Fall River, Massachusetts, numerous times a guest, though, she didn't expect part of the mystery surrounding the house to return with her to her apartment in Toronto, Canada.

The home, once owned by the infamous Lizzie Borden after the violent deaths of her father and stepmother, has kept its secrets since 1892. On that warm late-summer morning, Lizzie had slept in while her family readied for the day. Andrew J. Borden, a prosperous but cantankerous man, had left for work right after 9 o'clock, leaving his wife, Abby Durfee Gray Borden, at home with Lizzie and their maid, Bridget Sullivan, while his other daughter Emma was away visiting friends. What happened in the house next has puzzled theorists for over a hundred years.

After rising, Lizzie called down to the maid after entering the parlor at 11 o'clock, "Come down quick! Father's dead! Somebody's come in and killed him!" Andrew had been brutally beaten, his head shattered by an axe while sitting on the horsehair sofa. After sending Bridget to fetch the doctor across the street, Lizzie waited for their return. A next-door neighbor arrived to see what the commotion was about. It was then that the women discovered the body of Abby Borden in the guest room, face down on the rug, her body placed in a kneeling position next to the bed. She too had been viciously attacked by a person wielding a blunt instrument, receiving nineteen axe or hatchet blows to the back of her head. Though Andrew had been approached from behind, experts thought that Abby had seen her assailant before turning to run. Whose eyes bore into hers before the blows fell?

Lizzie was arrested for the crime, but was acquitted five weeks later. Borden remained in Falls River until she died in 1927, but at a price. While she did not serve jail time for the deaths of her parents, the community treated her as a pariah—was the stain of the murders imprinted on the house in way of a haunting? Many think so. Now converted into a bed-and-breakfast, guests have reported hearing a woman's sobs while other have seen objects moving or being tucked in at night by an older woman wearing a Victorian-era dress.

Repeat guest Sèphera Girón remembers a few occasions while spending the night there: "I've experienced all kinds of unexplainable events when I slept over at the Lizzie Borden Bed and Breakfast four times. There are 'cat ghosts' who rub against your legs, and if you end up actually trying to sleep and are lying on your stomach, they will jump on your back and 'knead' you. There are all kinds of dark energies. I never have so many orbs in pictures as I do when I photograph objects at the Lizzie Borden House."

During one of Girón's stays in 2007, the house was undergoing renovation. When seeing a pile of discarded lumber, she took a small piece of wood from what was once the original structure.

"I thought it would be a nice little souvenir. I didn't really think much of it except that I had a cool little piece of wood from a haunted house. When I moved from a house into a tiny apartment in 2010, everything was in disarray. I myself was in disarray as I was going through a heartbreaking divorce. However, I remember sitting in my new apartment one night and thinking about various things. I had put most of my stuff into a storage unit down the street, and I wondered where I had put my Lizzie Borden 'stick' and figured I would have to dig through boxes of my office stuff in the storage unit to find it. Somehow, it was at my feet, under my desk," she said.

"It creeped me out that I thought about it and then suddenly it was there. I now keep it on my desk where I can see it."

NO REST FOR THE CURIOUS: AUTHOR'S STORY

Driving up the narrow, winding mountain road, I was reminded of my favorite book, Shirley Jackson's *The Haunting of Hill House*, as we rounded the last curve into the driveway to face the heart-shaped lawn and the imposing structure of the retreat.

"Within, walls continued upright, bricks met neatly, floors were firm, and doors were sensibly shut; silence lay steadily against the wood and stone of Hill House, and whatever walked there, walked alone," Jackson writes.

This wasn't my first ghost rodeo. I'd been researching and writing about ghosts for over twenty years, so when offered the chance to spend the weekend with a handful of horror writers and have full run of a reportedly very haunted estate, I couldn't pass up the chance to dip my toes back into the paranormal. Leaving my home outside of Washington, DC. I traveled to San Francisco, hitching a ride with friends to the retreat in Mill Valley, a lovely village east of the larger city. One of my carmates had been to the retreat before. It was at his and writer Scott Browne's invitation that I was there at all—they promised me sunshine, great food, and all the ghosts I could shake a dowsing rod at.

As night fell on the first evening, the writers who had been there before swapped stories. Strange sounds and phantom touches had left them eager to see what the ghosts had in store for them this time. The house's history told of a time when the gold rush of California had given way to the timber barons of the surrounding hills outside of San Francisco. The owner of the property had come into his fortune in the early nineteenth century after inheriting his wealth when his father passed away, enabling him to start work on the sixteen-room mansion in the secluded hills of Mill Valley.

Boasting three stories and voluminous porches that stemmed from bedrooms overlooking redwood trees and hiking trails, the estate looked innocent in the daylight, but I couldn't shake the feeling that I—we—were being watched. While the manager of the property has not experienced his own brush with the paranormal, ghost stories have been rampant about the house that stood on the hill. The staff have seen visions of ghosts in the bedrooms, being pushed from behind by unseen forces, and have heard humming coming from one of the lower bedrooms where the original mistress of the house spent her final years. I couldn't wait to get started.

I was sharing a large room with my old friend Scott Browne, the writer of the zombie novel *Breathers*. Having also been at the retreat a few years before, he had experienced something in the room where we were to stay and was eager for me to see if I would also experience paranormal activity. Having regularly had my hair pulled, nose tweaked, and heavy breathing in my ear during investigations, I was ready for whatever these ghosts—in particular the one they had named Gretchen during an investigation during the prior retreat—had in their ghostly bag of tricks.

Describing what had happened at the last retreat, I wasn't as confident after I'd heard him tell the events of 2010 and sleeping in Gretchen's haunted bed.

"My first night at the Haunted Mansion Writer's Retreat, I slept in a single/twin bed, sharing the room with another person, who was sleeping in one of the other beds. Having gone to bed after midnight, I kept hearing sounds that kept me awake, so I slept restlessly. Twice, upon closing my eyes at different times, I felt the air around me grow thick and heavy, an atmospheric change in the room, but when I opened my eyes, all I saw was the room bathed in the ambient light from the next room and coming from the windows," Scott shared.

"Then, just before 5 a.m., I heard my roommate snoring and rolled over from my left to my right side and closed my eyes. Immediately I once more felt the air around me grow heavy, only this time much heavier and closer than before. At this point, I don't know if I opened my eyes first or felt something start to shake me, but the next moment, my eyes open and something is shaking me as if grabbing on to my left shoulder.

"Because of the ambient light coming into the room, I can see everything in clear detail. The bedroom door. My suitcase on a suitcase stand. The bed upon which I'm sleeping. And at the edge of the bed, directly in front of me, the air is dark and shimmering. It's shapeless, or appears so, but I can't be sure as I'm unable to look anywhere but directly in front of me. I can't look up or down. My gaze is frozen. I'm petrified. Unable to move. I can feel my dry lips and mouth, opening to shout out 'Hey' or say something to break the spell, but I can't speak.

"I don't know how long this goes on. Five seconds. Fifteen seconds. Half a minute. But either I finally manage to break the spell or else whatever is shaking me stops and leaves, and I sit up in bed and shout out 'Motherfucker' and look around. I don't see anything, so I grab the K2 EMF meter on the bedside table and turn it on, then wave it around to see if it picks up anything, but the light stays on green. I'm alone in the room, except for my roommate, who wakes up but doesn't say anything to me about the experience until the next morning."

All right. Maybe I jumped the gun a little in booking a room with an invisible wake-up service.

Scott eventually decided to try out sleeping on the third floor, rumored to have a ghost pacing angrily in the hallways, while I moved to a smaller room a few doors down and next to my friend, Steve. As jet lag claimed me, I slept in fits as waves of coldness washed over my face, though my body was warm. The ghost was checking the new girl out. Footsteps wandered the hallway, though I wasn't sure if they were from the other writers finding their way in unfamiliar hallways or if I had a tipsy ghost with unsteady feet. As the steps paused outside of my door, I whispered for them to go away—I would deal with them in the morning.

Soft daylight filtered in through the window over my head hours later. Meeting the other writers in the enormous sitting room, I barely glanced over my shoulder as I passed a man on the stairs. Later, I realized the mustachioed man wasn't one of our group, nor most likely had had a pulse for a number of years. It was beginning.

The day crept on as we each focused our attention on writing projects, with only one ear open for unusual sounds. Aside from the man on the stairs, I saw nothing and waited for nightfall. After dinner, we broke into groups to investigate the large house. Armed with my usual cadre of basic ghost hunting necessities: a digital voice recorder, flashlight, and a healthy dose of common sense, we began our electronic voice phenomena (EVP) sessions in different parts of the house. Some writers had come for ambience to inspire their works-in-progress; I wanted to see a floating head.

Unfortunately for me, there were neither whispers to be captured nor heads to be seen during the weekend. Though on the last morning, while waiting for the rest of the house to awake, I heard beneath my room the furious moving of furniture. It was 4:30 a.m., and I thought the staff was busy in the kitchen and the dining room: too busy—and definitely too busy for that hour of the morning. I listened to the sound of chairs being dragged across the floor and tables slamming in to one another for nearly ninety minutes. I heard glasses shattering against hard surfaces and wondered what the heck they were making for breakfast that required such enthusiasm.

Creeping out of my door at 6 a.m., I encountered Steve leaving his room. He hadn't heard a thing: he had been awoken by the sound of two women standing over him as he slept, then eavesdropped on their conversation. I had heard nothing of the sort in my room, but perhaps their whispers weren't meant for me.

Saying goodbye to our new comrades in haunting, we left the house and wound our way back to San Francisco along the same curvy roads we'd hurried along a few days earlier. This time we slowed down, each in thought as to our own experiences that defied reasonable explanation. Whatever remained in the house again walked alone.

EIGHT

TINSELTOWN

Some stars don't dim, they get snuffed out. Stories of actors who lived too fast and burned out too quickly litter the California landscape, leaving a bruise on the perfect face of Hollywood. Are these stories a cautionary tale about those with a wild side who held nothing back, or just another case of Hollywood heartbreak?

It's difficult to imagine James Dean without conjuring the image of him pressed against his beloved car, the Little Bastard, and his death along a stretch of road in the California desert, entwining his passing with what some regard as a curse. As the car and the man evolve into legend, we are left to ask: Are cars born bad? As Hollywood's elite die, some find that they're not ready to exit gracefully and remain attached to the material objects they grew fond of in life. For those who never made it into the ranks of stardom, they discovered that Hollywood is a jealous mistress: she wants everything—even after you're dead.

HOLLYWOOD SIGN

The promise of celebrity from its famous letters beckons young and hungry actors from around the world, but the Hollywood sign in California masks a darker side to fame. Constructed in 1923 on Mount Lee in Griffith Park, the fifty-foot-tall letters were an advertisement for a housing development financed by *Los Angeles Times* publisher Harry Chandler. Spelling out "HOLLYWOODLAND," the sign was less about the film industry than where to raise your kids outside of Los Angeles. Since everything is shinier in California, the sign was designed for maximum impact with thirty-foot-wide white letters and using 4,000 twenty-watt light bulbs to blind the heck out of anyone within viewing distance.

Though it was never meant to be used for more than a few years, the sign quickly fell into disrepair after the Great Depression forced cuts into its maintenance in 1939. The once-bright lights had been stolen or never replaced after burning out, and the sign itself fell victim to the whims of vandals by the end of the 1940s. Letters were toppling over due to high wind or their infrastructure stolen for scrap, and the sign reflected not only the hardship of its own struggle to remain strong in difficult times, but also that of its community. Battered and lonely, it refused to give up the fight. The Hollywood Chamber of Commerce commissioned the Los Angeles Parks Department to take over the care of the now-famous sign, deciding to remove the bulbs due to the cost of replacing them and dismantling the latter portion of the sign, leaving only what we recognize now as the famous Hollywood sign.

Thirty years passed. A generation of actors stared at the sign on the hill and wondered if they'd add their star to Hollywood's roster, though by the late 1970s the sign was again falling apart due to neglect. This time Hollywood took it personally. Funds were raised to sell the letters for $27,700 each, and the old sign was destroyed in order to construct the new version we see shining today.

PEG ENTWHISTLE

While the sign itself finally had a happy ending, Broadway actress Peg Entwhistle found more fame in her death than in her career. Leaving New York City in 1932, Entwhistle came to California after roles on the Broadway stage dried up. The Depression had robbed families of their financial ability to enjoy the theater, and they preferred the more affordable and accessible films. While successful on the East Coast, Entwhistle quickly blended in with the countless other actresses who had come to Hollywood on the promise of fame only to find parts were harder to land. Lucky to be contracted to a short-term deal with RKO Studios, Entwhistle landed a small role in the film *Thirteen Women*. Confident it would lead to larger parts, she looked forward to the film's release, only to discover her small supporting role had been cut to little more than a cameo.

Times were desperate. Without work, she couldn't afford to stay in California, yet she lacked the funds to return to New York. Staying with her uncle who lived in a house near the Hollywood sign, she left one evening for a walk to clear her head. It was during that walk in the cool evening hours in September 1932 that Entwhistle made her final decision. Climbing the hardscrabble hill toward the sign, she was resigned to no longer be a burden to her family, to her craft, or to herself. Finding a maintenance ladder propped up behind the letter H, she removed her coat and folded it neatly at the bottom of the imposing structure. Leaving her purse with a suicide note written inside, the young actress climbed to the top of the letter, stared out at the city that had crushed her will, and jumped.

The next morning, a hiker found her coat and purse, leaving it in the early morning hours at the police station. Entwhistle's body was found two days later, having rolled down the hill and into the brush. Two days after the body was recovered, Entwhistle's uncle received a letter for his niece—she had been chosen to star as the lead in a new production at the Beverly Hills Playhouse.

Today, the Hollywood sign is known for welcoming a new crop of hopeful actors to its sunny valley. Trails that cross Griffith Park and Beachwood Canyon come close to the sign, with some hikers reporting seeing a woman in 1930s-era clothing walking around the area only to vanish as they approach her. The police station has fielded calls about a young woman about to leap from the sign, though after searching the area they find no body—spectral or otherwise. There are some reports of visitors smelling the heady scent of gardenias near the sign, Peg Entwistle's favorite perfume. Has the residual haunting stained the lure of Hollywood or just added to the lore of the famous city?

JAMES DEAN AND THE LITTLE BASTARD

Just one look at the gorgeous silver convertible Porsche 550 Spyder and you knew it was trouble. Flaunting smooth, sexy curves, the car was supposed to handle like a champ on the raceways it was designed for, and actor James Dean couldn't resist its allure, naming it the Little Bastard. His friend, fellow actor Alec Guinness, warned him about the car, telling the actor the car would be the end of him and not to drive it. Dean didn't listen. On his way to a race in Salinas, California, on September 30, 1955, he and his mechanic Rolf Wutherich were involved in a head-on collision by a car driven by college student Donald Turnupseed, who made a sudden left turn in front of the Little Bastard. Taking the brunt of the collision, James Dean died while en route to the hospital of a broken neck and internal injuries.

After the accident, George Barris, the "King of Kustomizers," bought the wreck of the Little Bastard to sell for scrap, but the car was born bad and wasn't finished yet. While being transported to Barris's garage, the car slipped of its trailer, breaking a mechanic's leg. Later, Barris sold the engine to Troy McHenry and driveshaft to William Eschrid, both racecar drivers. During a race at Pomona Fairgrounds, not a month after the crash that took Dean's life, the men were subjected to the curse of the Little Bastard. McHenry was killed after his car took a curve too fast and hit a tree while Eschrid's car rolled over while going into a curve, saying the car "locked up on him."

Other incidents followed. While the car was in storage, thieves attempted to steal parts from it and one of the youth's arms was ripped open on the jutting metal as he tried to remove the steering wheel. Barris, putting it on loan to the California Highway Patrol to promote highway safety, didn't count on the car's unlucky residue. The garage where the wreckage was stored went up in flames one night, destroying everything but the car itself. Later, while on display at Sacramento High School, the car fell and resulted in a student breaking his hip.

Even moving the Little Bastard was dangerous. On its way to Salinas, the truck carrying the car lost control; the driver, having been flung out of the cab of the truck, was crushed by Dean's vehicle when it fell off the back. Apparently it didn't enjoy being tied down; the Porsche came loose and came off the back of other transportation trucks twice more.

Its last public exhibit was for the Highway Patrol in 1959 when the wreckage collapsed into pieces. Loaded onto a boxcar to travel to Los Angeles and permanent retirement, the car had one last surprise. After the train arrived, Barris removed the seal from the boxcar and opened the heavy doors to see…nothing. The Little Bastard had vanished.

SWASHBUCKLING SPOOKS: ERROL FLYNN'S INFAMOUS *ZACA*

Tasmanian Lothario and actor Errol Flynn burst onto the Hollywood scene in 1935 with his role as Captain Blood, a character who linked his love of the sea to his burgeoning film career. But as his wicked ways off screen wove into the legend of his yacht, the *Zaca*, Flynn's hard partying lifestyle left an indelible impression on the boat and all she came in contact with after his death in 1959.

Purchasing the 118-foot gaff-rigged schooner in 1945 from Joe Rosenberg after the luxury yacht had been decommissioned following World War II, Flynn was ready to take his infamous parties on the wild sea. Tales of orgies, drinking, and underage ladies scampering about the hardwood decks leaked to the mainland, cementing the actor's reputation as a ladies' man who mimicked the heroes of his movies. As Flynn's health deteriorated, however, the film roles dried up and he was forced to try to sell his beloved *Zaca*. While in Vancouver, British Columbia, and preparing to lease the yacht to millionaire George Caldough, Flynn fell ill during a party and later suffered a fatal heart attack.

Flynn's wife at the time, Patrice Wymore, was still living aboard the boat. Due to finances, she was left with little choice but to sell the boat quickly to Freddie Tinsley, who swore he would restore the *Zaca* to shipshape while berthed in France. After the *Zaca* was docked in Ville-franche, though, it was stripped and left to rot. However, the party wasn't quite over.

An owner of a neighboring yacht told stories of hearing music coming from the darkened ship. Women's laughter skipped along the quiet water and teased the ears of those lucky enough to witness the last of Flynn's famous parties. For the next twenty years, there were multiple reports of seeing the actor pacing the decks at twilight.

In 1979, the shipyard owner had taken control of the *Zaca* for nonpayment of rent by Tinsley, but before he could begin work to rebuild the once lovely ship, he wanted to toss out the ghostly squatters. But having a Catholic priest and an Anglican Archdeacon perform an exorcism on a yacht was no simple task. Instead, a model of the ship was taken to a church in Monte Carlo and accompanied by several witnesses to the haunting. After the ceremony, there ceased to be any further paranormal parties. The *Zaca* has now been restored and is once more cutting through the waves, as her swashbuckling captain would have always wished.

THE GOOSING CHAIR OF CLIFTON WEBB

Actor Clifton Webb was sure his house was haunted. In fact, he embraced the idea of his mother's spirit remaining with him as she did during his life—always supportive, always nurturing, and slightly smothering. The two had been inseparable since his birth in 1889. Leaving her husband to care for and protect her son while he was a toddler, Maybelle wasn't about to let Webb go off half-cocked now that she was no longer there to direct his future—and he liked it that way.

Webb began his acting career early. He was on the New York stage by the age of seven as part of the New York Children's Theater group and perfected his persona as being snobbish and condescending throughout the years, eventually landing him roles in Hollywood in films such as *Laura*, for which he earned an Academy Award nomination, and *The Razor's Edge*. Webb became best known, however, for his role as Mr. Belvedere, an uptight author who took on the role of a nanny for three children as research for his upcoming book. The roles gained him fame and a fortune to spend on Maybelle, who was forever by his side.

Later, when the opportunity arose to buy a house once owned by actor Gene Lockhart, Webb jumped on it, as he'd always admired the home. After Maybelle died in 1960, Webb held séances to try to contact his mother as well as his friend, Grace Moore, whom he had seen as a ghost in the house multiple times. A firm believer in the afterlife, Webb was content to open up the paranormal channels to communicate with those in the otherworld and once again content himself that Maybelle was never far away.

Webb lived in the house for twenty years, becoming more and more of a recluse after Maybelle's passing, until his death in 1966 from heart failure. A year later, a television producer and his wife, a columnist who wrote for the *Los Angeles Times*, moved in to the house only to experience visions of Webb wandering the rooms, rustling the curtains, staring at the poor woman through the window. Webb's favorite room, dubbed the "Greek Room" because of its Grecian theme, had been made into a guest room by the couple. Visitors were subjected to Webb's peculiar welcome of locking them in the bathroom, crushing cigarettes on their beds or tossing the cigarette package across the room (he was notoriously intolerant of smoking), and being quite possessive over a favorite chair. Whenever a woman sat in his old armchair, the chair reportedly bounced and made odd sounds, presumably in an effort for her to remove her posterior from the upholstery. My word.

THE JINXED RING OF RUDOLPH VALENTINO

Women couldn't help themselves as the man with the dark eyes—and darker secrets—stared down their early twentieth-century inhibitions and ignited a frenzy at the box office. Rudolph Valentino carried away the hearts of thousands, starring in silent films such as *The Sheik* (1921) and *The Four Horsemen of the Apocalypse* (1921), but what brought the fabled "Latin Lover" to his death in 1926 at the age of thirty-one?

Valentino was born Rodolfo Alfonso Raffaello Pierre Filibert Guglielmi di Valentina d'Antonguolla in Italy to the daughter of a French surgeon and an Italian veterinarian in 1895. Coming to America right before Christmas in 1913, Valentino found work as a taxi dancer, or dancer for hire, at Maxim's in New York City. His mastery of the Argentine tango introduced the dance to a wider audience in his later film work. While he swept the floor with the city's society ladies, however, he had his eye on a bigger prize.

Moving to California, he had bit parts in films by 1914, though usually cast as the villain due to his dark looks. Heroes of the day were typically viewed as blond with a fair complexion; Valentino strove to change the way women reacted to a man with more exotic features. He did—with a vengeance. *The Sheik*, released in 1921, solidified his reputation as the intense, dark-eyed lover women had been waiting for. The film was an enormous success and cemented his status as a major film star.

So how did a man who, though unlucky in his own love life, seemed to have everything at the tips of his fingers fall so quickly? In 1920, Valentino dropped in at a jewelry shop in San Francisco, California. The legend tells that while the jeweler warned the actor that the ring had a dark history, the silver ring, which was decorated with semiprecious stones, intrigued Valentino enough to purchase it without another thought. Valentino was known for his over-the-top tastes in jewelry and furs: How could a small ring bring him any harm?

When he wore the ring during the filming of *The Young Rajah*, it became linked to the biggest flop of his career. Refusing to wear it again until using it as a prop while filming *The Son of the Sheik*, he again became accustomed to having the ring back on his finger. Three weeks after wrapping the film, he suffered an acute attack of appendicitis and gastric ulcers. After surgery, he developed peritonitis and perished on August 23, 1926. His fans were devastated. It is estimated that thousands of people lined the streets of New York City during his funeral, some even committing suicide after the memorial.

Later, actress and claimed fiancée of Valentino, Pola Negri, inherited the silver ring. Soon after taking possession of the ring, Negri fell into a serious illness that halted her film career. A year later, she gave the ring to a young singer whom she felt resembled Valentino, Russ Columbo.

A few days later, Columbo was dead, the victim of a freak shooting accident. His cousin gave Valentino's ring to Joe Casino, Columbo's best friend. Aware that there may be more to the ring than decoration, Casino put it away in a case and forgot about it. Years passed and Casino discovered the ring once more. Trying to forget the foolishness of rumored jinxes, he placed the ring on his finger. A week later, he was dead—the victim of a hit-and-run driver. Casino's brother then came into possession of the ring, and while he never wore it, the ring was stolen from his house. The thief was shot and killed by police as he left the house, the ring still on his body. The last victim of the cursed ring was an actor who wore the ring while filming a biographical film about the fallen star. During the two weeks of wearing the ring, he was diagnosed and died of a rare blood disease. The ring now sits in a safety deposit box in Los Angeles.

Was the ring truly cursed as the jeweler had predicted or was it a bizarre set of circumstances that led to the downfall of young, seemingly healthy people? As Valentino's ghost has been seen multiple places around Hollywood, it may not be that far-fetched to think he's put a little mojo back in a little band of silver.

PUCKER UP: MONROE'S MIRROR

Marilyn Monroe's print career was launched from the diving board of the famous Roosevelt Hotel in Hollywood, California. While posing for a toothpaste ad in the 1940s alongside the pool, Monroe grew fond of the glamorous hotel and often stayed there during the 1950s as her career grew. After her death in August 1962, Monroe's favorite full-length dark-framed mirror was moved to the manager's office.

Following a two-year restoration of the property in 1985, the Roosevelt Hotel was ready to shine once more and rejoin Hollywood's elite hotels as a place to see and be seen. Readying the mirror for its eventual placement in a hotel elevator foyer, employee Suzanne Leonard noticed a blond figure of a woman in the reflection behind her. Turning to greet the woman, there was no one there, though her reflection still registered on the surface of the large mirror. Later, Ms. Leonard learned that the mirror was once in Monroe's favorite room. Since installing the mirror, there have been reports of people seeing what they believe is the ghost of Marilyn Monroe trapped within the cold glass.

NINE

JINXES

What if that doll giving you the stink-eye isn't just an object on a misplaced mission of hate? What if the doll had a purpose? A deliberate curse infused into an item then given or passed onto another is called a jinx.

At the online marketplace, Etsy, homemade cures are available to rid whatever curse stuck to your shoe and now makes your life miserable. The site offers everything from soaps and candles to herbs, spell kits, and bat's blood–colored ink to help rid the afflicted of bad luck. If one needs a little backup, spellcasters are waiting for an email to help rid one from the hex. No matter one's belief in jinxes, real or imagined, the psychological effects of jinxes can be devastating to those who feel they are under attack. Sometimes the power of suggestion is the most damaging of all.

NO ROAMIN' FOR THESE ROMANS

Ancient Romans weren't taking any chances. Believing ghosts could take revenge on others after the body grew cold, a piece of lead or pewter inscribed with a curse was occasionally placed in the grave. The jinx would disturb the spirit until the hexer's wishes were carried out. Only then would the ghost be able to rest.

In an article for *Discovery.com*, writer Rossella Lorenzi described the archaeological finding of hundreds of curse tablets left by the Romans around Great Britain. With these being common in the Greek and Roman civilizations, the curser would scratch the hex upon a scroll or a small lead tablet and would usually bury it in places where the underworld could find it: graves or wells. The tablets were also nailed onto the walls of temples; the writers weren't bashful in seeking revenge against those whom they'd felt wronged them. One scroll found in the thermal springs of the British city of Bath read, "Tretia Maria and her life and mind and memory and liver and lungs mixed up together, and her words, thoughts and memory." I think someone needs a hug.

VICTORIAN DOLL: NOW WITH EXTRA CURSES

Tucked away in a crevice of a brick wall of a house in Hereford, England, was a Victorian-era wooden doll with an attitude. Its limbs were made of a red checked cotton material, while the head is a nightmare of soft fabric with traces of paint on its frowning face, string, and a braided silk pigtail dangling off the left side of its head. The doll's dress was a voluminous balloon of red spots on a navy blue background, hiding the feet, and hidden away with the folds was a curse from one very upset lady.

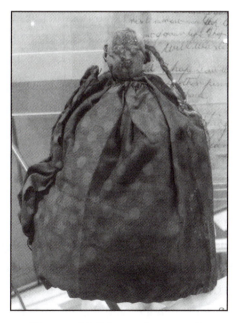

The cursed doll that can be seen at the
Herefordshire Museum. Courtesy of Lucy Cheung.

Now housed at the Herefordshire Museum, the doll is displayed with its accompanying note with the wish that Mary Ann would never rest, sleep, or eat for the remainder of her life—with the added venom of hoping the woman's flesh would be eaten away as a sassy touch.

THE HEART-SHAPED CURSE

The air was tinted with spice, and exotic sights awaited the influx of travelers to Egypt's famous pyramids after archaeologist Howard Carter unveiled the wonders of King Tutankhamun's tomb to the world in 1922. Eager to be part of the privileged crowd to tour the desert ruins in 1936, Sir Alexander "Sandy" Hay Seton, the 10th Baron of Abercom, and his wife, Zeyla, traveled from Edinburgh to Cairo. Did one act of grave robbery result in a destructive haunting and contribute to the end a marriage?

Touring the area with their guide Abdul, the couple entered a newly opened tomb of a young woman that was found behind the great pyramids. Descending down the rough stones into the tomb, the group discovered the remains of a pre-mummy era body lying on a stone slab. The tomb itself had been filled with mud from the Nile at one time, preserving the corpse, about five thousand years ago. After the river receded, it took part of the body with it, leaving the skull, leg bones, and the spine with a few spindly ribs intact and ready for viewing by curious onlookers in the nineteenth century. As the tour members took their fill of the dark tomb, Seton was more than ready to escape back into the daylight. Zeyla, fascinated with the skeleton, hung back from the rest of the party, asking for one more look before returning to the hot sand outside.

According to Seton's unpublished autobiography, *The Transgressions of a Baronet*, Zeyla begged off from stopping at a souvenir shop on the way back to their hotel, telling her husband that she had a much better memento from their trip. She showed him a heart-shaped bone she had removed from the skeleton in the tomb. Aghast, Seton told her to put it away and thought nothing more of it until they returned to Scotland.

During a dinner party weeks later, their trip was discussed and Zeyla ran to find the bone to show her friends. Placing it in a former clock case, the bone was passed around and shown as a "grotesque relic." As their friends left that evening, the Setons were nearly crushed by a large piece of the roof parapet when it crashed to the ground two feet away as they said goodbye to their guests. Coincidence? Perhaps.

Leaving the case in the drawing room, they went to bed shaken. Not long afterward, their daughter's nanny alerted them to hearing noises coming from a room and suspected an intruder. After checking out the room and helping the nanny calm down, they found nothing. The next morning, the bone was found on the floor with the case lying on its side. Righting the box, they thought nothing more of the bone until a few nights later when the noises started again. Seton's young nephew, Alasdair Black, told the family one morning of getting up in the middle of the night only to see "a funny-dressed person going upstairs," but after a night watching for activity, Seton could come up with no explanation. Time passed and the mysterious noises started again, but this time when they inspected the room, heavy furniture had been tipped over and the bone was back on the floor. Making the connection of the upheaval with the stolen Egyptian bone, Seton told his wife he was going to burn it and a fight ensued. Zeyla was excited by the thought of having a haunted bone to show off to her friends, why destroy it?

Leaving the house, Seton retreated to his club, where, after a few drinks, he told his friends of the bone and what trouble it was making at his house. That night when he returned, the table on which the case rested had been shattered. The story told at the club was leaked to a reporter who shared it with the world. News agencies hounded the family for details about what was happening, but there was no more to tell them until weeks later. While he was away from the house, his nanny told him of how the room sounded as if it was again destroyed by unseen hands. This time when he entered the room, he found the room was in order—except for the table that lay on its side, the broken glass of the case, and the bone that was now broken into five pieces.

On Boxing Day, the Setons held a dinner party to celebrate the holiday. Friends who had heard of the heart-shaped bone were curious to see it and asked if there had been any other phenomena. A friend of Zeyla's, a doctor, mended the bone as well as he could and placed it on a table leading into the dining room. While the guests enjoyed their drinks, the table flew across the space and hit the opposite wall, emitting a large thump. It's not a party until a cursed bone demands attention, people. More drinks were needed.

The story spread as guests returned from the party and news of the bone reached an even greater audience. Seton started receiving letters, one of which, he claimed, was from archaeologist Howard Carter that told him that things like this could happen, had happened, and would go on happening. Seton had had enough.

Calling on the help of his uncle, a monk from the Fort Augustus Abbey, Seton was ready to have the bone exorcised and destroyed. Father Benedict arrived while Zeyla was gone and performed the ceremony before she returned, possibly to save himself from the woman's wrath of having her social centerpiece taken away. Seton then burned the bone and hoped the paranormal activity was gone forever.

In his memoir, he said this: "My own interpretation of the matter is that through some uncanny power of religion it was brought under destructive control but if—and I emphasise the world 'if'—it really did carry a curse, as many people thought, the curse certainly did not end when I destroyed the Bone by fire, and from 1936 onwards trouble, sometimes grave, seemed to be always around the corner." The last straw in an already troubled marriage, Zeyla and Seton divorced afterward.

FRENCH BLUE: THE CURSE OF THE HOPE DIAMOND

Known for a trail of notorious deaths and misery, the Hope Diamond's past is still hidden behind the shadowy veil of time. Unequal in size at 112.5 carats and its deep blue beauty, the diamond bewitched those unlucky enough to afford its ill-gotten elegance. Its legend began in 1642 when plucked from the forehead (or eye) of the Indian goddess Sita by a Hindu priest and smuggled into Europe by French jeweler Jean-Baptiste Tavernier. Purchased by Louis XIV of France in 1668, the gem was re-cut to enhance its swagger and was known as the "French Blue" or the "Blue Diamond of the Crown," to be worn around the king's neck suspended by a ribbon.

Evalyn Walsh McLean wearing the Hope Diamond
in the early 1900s. Courtesy of the Library of Congress.

Now the legend gets juicy. Rumor swirled around Europe that after selling the huge jewel, Tavernier traveled to Russia and was mauled by wolves, resulting in his horrifying death. In reality, the jeweler died at the age of eighty-four after moving to Russia. It is not known if wolves had any part in his demise; however, the first faint whisperings of the curse had taken hold.

After the death of Louis XIV, also called the Sun King, the diamond eventually passed to his heirs, Louis XVI and his wife, Marie Antoinette. They had an unfortunate parting of their heads from their shoulders during the revolution, as did a lady of the court who had worn the diamond. Princess de Lamballe was torn apart by French mobs, her head reportedly impaled upon a spike and carried to Marie Antoinette's window before the queen's death. A succession of owners brought new tales of woe: the Dutch jeweler Wilhelm Fals had the diamond re-cut, later being robbed and murdered by his son, and George IV of England died mad and deeply in debt, with the diamond being sold to pay off his obligations. The diamond came to rest within the holdings of British banker Henry Thomas Hope around 1830. Giving the now-famous gem its name, Hope had no idea that his family too would succumb to the curse of the blue diamond as their fortune dwindled, leading the diamond to once again be sold after his death to numerous owners.

Subsequent owners included Prince Ivan Kanitovski and his lover, Mademoiselle Lorens Ladue. After having Ladue murdered, Kanitovski himself was killed by Russian revolutionaries. Abdul Hamid II, the Sultan of Turkey, purchased the diamond for $400,000 in 1908 for his favorite concubine, Surbaya, but promptly received it back after having her stabbed to death a year later. Hamid was later deposed as Sultan after the Turkish uprising.

The Hope Diamond came into the possession of famed jeweler Pierre Cartier in the early nineteenth century. Seeking a wealthy buyer for such a rare item, Cartier showed the Hope Diamond to Evalyn Walsh McLean in Paris in 1910. After first rejecting it due to its setting, McLean eventually purchased the diamond believing it would bring her good luck instead of the unhappiness it seemed to bring in its wake. Unfortunately, the diamond may have struck once again with the death of both of her children at early ages, the end of her marriage, and the eventual sale of the diamond by her heirs to pay off McLean's extravagant lifestyle.

Sold in 1949 to Harry Winston, the jeweler donated the Hope Diamond to the Smithsonian Institution to support his cause of establishing a national gem collection in 1958. The diamond wouldn't go quietly, however. Delivered in a plain brown paper package to the museum, the deliveryman, James Todd, would later suffer the loss of his house to fire, a head injury during an automobile accident, and the crushing of his leg in a truck accident.

Is the jewel cursed or were the former owners just unlucky? Most of the "curses" may be attributed to outrageous circumstances, but who are we to doubt the winking eye of a Hindu goddess?

Conclusion

Whether a haunted hodgepodge or just creepy clutter, we're finding more haunted stuff every day as the living become more in tune with our paranormal counterparts. The shuffle between our mortal coil and the otherworld may be getting less distinct and leaves a tiny bit of wiggle room in which ghosts can come back to visit the items they left behind. Those stories passed down through generations may not be old wives' tales after all, especially if the old wife is still fond of the rocker you inherited sitting in your living room.

As we lean in and listen—really listen—we discover more about the unseen world. Are ghosts a rip in dimensions or the product of an overactive imagination? Can energy choose where to place itself without the benefit of a body or can it settle in a cozy spot and wait for someone to pay attention? As we explore more about haunted objects, we allow ourselves to scrape away the mundane and see what lies beneath. Our curiosity is never sated and our journey has only begun to discover how the otherworld interacts with the living.

Thank you for joining me in the pages of *Haunted Stuff: Demonic Dolls, Screaming Skulls, and Other Creepy Collectibles.* Remember to stay curious, keep an open mind, and ask the questions we're afraid of the answer to—what we find is definitely worth a few sleepless nights.

APPENDIX:

How did our ancestors protect themselves from ghosts?

Every culture has its method of dealing with the afterlife. Some fear the unknown while others celebrate it, but many of them just want the ghost to stay put after being left in a pleasant graveyard away from the house. How can you protect your home from becoming a pit stop on the way to purgatory? Try these techniques plucked from history and around the world:

Iron: Often referred to as "cold iron" because it is cool to the touch, this metal has a long history of repelling spirits. Decorative iron fences around graveyards were meant to keep spirits locked within while a rod of iron placed on the grave added a little extra protection that a phantom wouldn't rise from its resting spot and return to see what was for dinner. Horseshoes not only brought luck to the homeowner if nailed over a door; the iron wards off any wandering ghosts that want to pop in for a chat.

Salt: Being a pure substance from the Earth, salt is traditionally believed to cleanse items and surroundings. Carrying a bit in your pocket not only protects you from ghosts, but also ensures that you're ready in case you run across underseasoned French fries. A line of salt sprinkled on doorways and windows guards against malevolent spirits entering and making a ruckus. Bowls of salt placed within the house may help dispel a ghost who is reluctant to move or rid the area of residual paranormal activity. Any type of salt may be used, but sea salt and kosher are recommended.

Rowan tree: A cross of rowan wood bound with red thread and sewn between the lining and outer cloth of a person's clothing would protect the wearer from any ghostly shenanigans. In the eighteenth century, the Highlanders of Scotland would hang the tree's branches festooned with wreaths of flowers over the doors of their homes to ward off unwanted supernatural visitors. Scottish women were also known to wear necklaces of rowan berries tied with red string as protection against evil spirits. Welsh churches planted the trees around the graveyard to watch over and protect the spirits of the dead. Further to the north, a rowan tree was planted directly on top of the grave to keep the body (and spirit) from haunting the family.

Haint paint: The belief that ghosts cannot travel over bodies of water helped create the unique blue shade found on many former slave homes in South Carolina and Georgia. By mixing a combination of lime, milk, and whatever pigments they could find that would mimic the blue sea into a pit dug into the soil, they would cover all openings into the home with the haint paint, including doors, window shutters, and porch ceilings in an effort to confuse mischievous spirits and stop them dead in their tracks.

Spirit houses: The Southeast Asian tradition of building spirit houses to honor and appease the spirits that influence daily lives can be seen in nearly every Thai household and business. A small structure is built and placed within the yard of homeowners, often mimicking the houses it resides near, and decorated with symbols and various figurines such as animals and people. A long wraparound porch may be attached to hold candles, incense, and a place for flowers. Some spirit houses are large enough to walk into, depending on which spirit the builder is hoping to attract, such as the Phra Bhum Jowthee, or Guardian Spirits of the Land, with each offering a different level of protection for the family. Offerings to the spirits often consist of flowers, betel leaves, fowl, and candles. This helps ensure the spirits of nature and those who have passed before them into death look favorably onto the household.

Going up! 10…11…12…14?: High-rise buildings may jump floors. Since in some cultures, ghosts can only live on the thirteenth floor due to its unlucky nature, builders tend to "skip" anything associated with the number. Next time you're on an elevator in a tall building, check and see if they've left off the cursed floor.

Just as Americans shy away from the number thirteen, Southeast Asians abhor the four. Some buildings have no fourth floor and may even skip all subsequent floors ending in the number.

Curved rooflines: The Buddhist belief that since ghosts can only travel in straight lines, a fluid curve of a roof makes it especially difficult for a pesky ghost to take up residence. Think of it as a roller coaster for the spirit world.

Ghost walls: The Chinese are taking nothing for granted. If a phantom has wiggled its way into a

home, it is faced with a protective "ghost wall."
When visitors arrive, they are forced to veer slightly
to either side, something a ghost cannot do and is
forced to retreat.

Curved driveways: Along the same lines as the roof,
curved driveways confuse ghosts and send them wandering off, making pizza delivery for the dead a challenge.

Basement exit for ghosts: And you thought it was the
furnace making all that noise. Some homeowners in
the Philippines believe that ghosts forgo the attic and
hang out below the house in the basement. In order
to prevent the ghosts from roaming the upper levels
of the house, the owners have a separate exit dug out
from beneath the basement for their spectral visitors
to use instead.

Northeast corner of the house: The Japanese believe
that in this direction lay the Kimon or "Devil's
Gate." To protect themselves from spiritual shenanigans, no entrances, windows, doors, or bathrooms
would be built in the northeast corner of a house.
The source of whatever misfortune befalls a family,
this is where evil spirits emanate from. The last thing
you need is a ghost in your bathroom plumbing.

Plants: Violets planted around homes in Greece or houseleeks on the roof can stop a ghost from making a mess, while the Aztecs believed that jimson weed would repel supernatural activity in any area where it grew. Scott Cunningham, in his book *The Magical Household: Spells and Rituals for the Home*, suggested filling an old sock with salt, sage, mullein, tansy, and other protective herbs and burying it under the front porch to keep ghosts away. Or scatter dill with salt, mullein, or fennel around the places you believe ghosts are hiding, as apparently they don't like to be well seasoned.

Garlic hung on the door isn't just for toothy vampires—it may be an effective way to get a ghost to leave you alone. Nail a wreath of garlic by your front door. If you feel a paranormal Peeping Tom is bothering you, take a bite of a clove and throw it away—the ghost will follow it instead of hanging around the house.

Door Gods: Portraits of Chinese generals, Qin Shubao and Yuchi Jingde, face either side of a doorway to a temple, home, or business, as a warning to ghosts that the occupants won't put up with their nonsense. Dating to the Tang Dynasty, the tradition began with Emperor Tang Taizong, who had paintings done of his most trusted and fiercest generals. After the emperor hung them outside his own palace doors, his subjects followed suit to hopefully attract good luck while scaring away evil spirits.

This glass sphere is called the globe of happiness, but some refer to it as a witch ball.
Courtesy of LaMishia Allen Photography.

The Globe of Happiness: Otherwise known as a witch ball, they were first fashioned in eighteenth-century Europe to ward off evil spirits. Usually hung in the east window to catch the morning sun's first rays, the balls are traditionally made of green or blue glass, though there are reports of others constructed from wood, grass, or small sticks with swirls of glass strung within the globe. Legend tells of how the balls were used to lure evil spirits with their bright colors, trapping them inside as the ghost tangled itself within the strands. Now seen as a more decorative item, witch balls are still thought to capture ghosts with sticky fingers.

Objects hidden in walls: Cats, shoes, and even clothing, it's an ancient belief that by entombing an item within the walls of your house, the occupants are protected from the influence of nasty spirits as well as witches. Funeral director Richard Parson told the British newspaper *The Telegraph* in April 2009 of finding the 400-year-old mummy of a cat within the walls of his house after renovation started: "Apparently 400 years ago people put cats behind walls to ward off witches. It clearly works as, since we have lived in the village, we have not seen sight or sound of any witches." It must work for ghosts as well.

Shoes were thought to be the only article of clothing to retain the shape of their owner after they were removed. Placing a shoe, usually that of a child, within the walls of a house was meant to guard the family as well as ensure good luck. Why a child's shoe? Usually the shoes cost less to make and children grow out of them more quickly. With a distinct lack of consignment stores 600 years ago, it was an easy way to recycle while keeping ghosts at bay. Recent theories are that the purity of children would deter any evil shenanigans a spirit may try to inflict upon the household. A small shoe was found in the Sydney Harbour Bridge in Australia recently, tells a story online from the BBC. Historian Ian Evans said this about the placement of the shoe in an access tunnel near the famous Opera House in the 1920s: "It was concealed by a builder or stone-mason to protect against evil forces."

Clothing stashed away under the eaves may be more than a reluctance to do laundry. As some items keep the smell of a human longer than others, it may have been thought to protect the household from unwanted spirits. The Deliberately Concealed Garments Project, online at concealedgarments.org, is a research database filled with these found objects. Caches of hats, shoes, and undergarments have been found throughout Great Britain, hidden away in hopes of keeping a curious ghost out of the attic.

Amulets and talismans: As cultures developed, each had their own system of dealing with the other-world and how to control those frisky spirits. Some chose to use gemstones such as amethyst, obsidian, or quartz, believing that the only thing that could counteract the wayward advances of a ghost was by using the Earth in its purest form. Others carried silver. Thought as a way to protect themselves from ghosts, the Miao people in southwest China cover themselves with as much as possible by way of jewelry, clothing items, and headdresses. It is their belief that after you die, there are three separate ghosts: one to stay at the tomb, another to travel to the ancestors, and a third that, if the death was unexpected or caused by an accident, may roam the streets and cause trouble with the living.

Acknowledgments

One of the best parts of writing a book like this is meeting the fabulous individuals who shared their stories and photographs with me: a huge thank you to Theresa and Todd Apple, Scott Browne, Morrighan Lynne, Brian McKavanagh, Nancy Reynolds, Sandi Rowe, Lucy Cheung, Gill Hoffs, Sèphera Girón, and Suzanne Kraus Mancuso. Your contributions brought *Haunted Stuff* to life.

I'd like to thank my agent, Dawn Frederick, for never batting an eye when I come up with crazy book ideas; and my editor, Amy Glaser, and the fantastic team at Llewellyn for their help in the process of bringing you *Haunted Stuff: Demonic Dolls, Screaming Skulls & Other Creepy Collectibles*.

A personal thank you to my husband, Bryan, and my daughters, Rowyn, Syenna, Wynter, Lily, and Vyolette, for endless nights of pizza and questionable housekeeping skills while I wrote this book; and Melanie Swiftney, Jason Tudor, and Angie Mansfield for their never-ending support. I'd like to add a very special thank you to Beth Bartlett for her mad proxy interviewing skills and keeping me on track when I wanted to hide under my desk and eat crackers.

BIBLIOGRAPHY

Addy, Sidney Oldall. "Traditional Remains." *Household Tales with Other Traditional Remains: Collected in the Counties of York, Lincoln, ...* (S.l.): Hardpress, 2013.

Allison, Andrea. "The Curse of James Dean's Car." *Ghost Stories: Collections of Stories About Paranormal Phenomena.* May 20, 2007.

———. "Mandy the Doll." *Ghost Stories: Collections of Stories About Paranormal Phenomena.* August 25, 2010.

"America's Most Haunted Hotel." *Americas Most Haunted Hotel.* http://www.americasmosthauntedhotel.com/.

"Annabelle." *The New England Society for Psychic Research.* http://www.warrens.net/Annabelle.html.

Antier, Cheryl. "French Riviera Haunted Places: Errol Flynn's Yacht—the Zaca." *Examiner.com.* N.p., October 24, 2009.

Aveni, Anthony F. *Behind the Crystal Ball: Magic, Science, and the Occult from Antiquity through the New Age*. New York: Times Books, 1996.

Beal, Matti. "Haunted Dolls and Why We Hate Them." *The Spooky Isles*. The Spooky Isles.

Belanger, Jeff. "L'Empire De La Mort." *The Catacombs of Paris, France*. Ghostvillage.com. October 4, 2003.

"Belcourt Castle." *HauntedHouses.com*.

Bowman, Susanne. "Aunt Pratt…Shirley's Own Ghost." *The Free Lance-Star* (Fredericksburg, VA). September 6, 1975. Town and Country sec.: 13–14.

Broome, Fiona. "Spiritual Protection for Ghost Hunters." *Spiritual Protection for Ghost Hunters*. Hollow Hill. April 12, 2008.

Brown, Alan. "The Driskill Hotel." *The Big Book of Texas Ghost Stories*. Mechanicsburg, PA: Stackpole, 2012.

Buckland, Raymond. *The Weiser Field Guide to Ghosts: Apparitions, Spirits, Spectral Lights, and Other Hauntings of History and Legend*. San Francisco: Weiser, 2009.

"Burton Agnes Hall: The Ghost." *Burton Agnes Hall*. http://www.burtonagnes.com/The_Hall/The_Ghost.html.

Butterworth-McKittrick, Norma Elizabeth, and Bruce Roberts. *Lighthouse Ghosts: 13 Bona Fide Apparitions Standing Watch over America's Shores*. Birmingham, AL: Crane Hill, 1999.

"Calgarth Hall." *Variety Portal*. www.varietyportal.com/calgarth-hall/ (site suspended).

Christensen, Jo-Anne. "Mandy: Quesnel's Haunted Doll." *Ghost Stories of British Columbia*. Toronto: Hounslow, 1996.

"Crosses of Rowan-Tree Used as Charms." *Crosses of Rowan-Tree Used as Charms*. ElectricScotland.com.

Cunningham, Scott, and David Harrington. *The Magical Household: Spells & Rituals for the Home*. St. Paul, MN: Llewellyn Publications, 2003.

"Curse of the Mary Celeste." Ghost Ships of the World. October 11, 2011.

"Curse of the Mummy." *Scotsman.com*. Johnston Publishing, Ltd. April 21, 2005.

"The Cursed Ring." *Unsolved Mysteries of the World*. Unsolved Mysteries of the World. May 10, 2010.

"The Cursed Skull of Tunstead Farm." *Ludchurch*.

"Dark Destinations—The Hollywood Sign." *TheCabinet.com*. Dark Destinations.

Davis, Jefferson. *Ghosts and Strange Critters of Washington and Oregon*. Vancouver, WA: Norseman Ventures, 1999.

"Deliberately Concealed Garments | Discover Items Which Have Been Hidden or Buried in Buildings." *Deliberately Concealed Garments*. Arts and Humanities Research Council.

"The Driskill Hotel: Historic Texas Hotels." *Downtown Austin Hotels*.

Ellis, Melissa Martin. *The Everything Ghost Hunting Book: Tips, Tools, and Techniques for Exploring the Supernatural World*. Avon, MA: Adams Media, 2009.

Elvis. "Ghost Culture in China." *Orichinese*. Orichinese. April 15, 2012.

"Etna Furnace." *Blair County Historical Society*. http://www.blairhistory.org/visit/historic-sites/etna-furnace/.

Farnsworth, Cheri. "Lizzie Borden House." *Haunted Massachusetts: Ghosts and Strange Phenomena of the Bay State*. Mechanicsburg, PA: Stackpole, 2005.

"The Fate of Theodosia Burr." *Coastal Guide*. http://www.coastalguide.com/packet/theodosiaburrmystery.shtml.

"Flatmates Put 'Haunted Mirror' up for Sale on Ebay after Being Dogged by Bad Luck, Financial Misery and Illness since Rescuing It from Dumpster." *Mail Online*. Daily Mail. February 19, 2013.

Floyd, E. Randall. *More Great Southern Mysteries: Florida's Fountain of Youth, Ghosts of the Alamo, Lost Maidens of the Okefenokee, Terror on the Natchez Trace, and Other Enduring Mysteries of the American South*. Little Rock: August House, 1990.

"The Flying Dutchman: Facts and Legends." *HubPages*. HubPages, Inc.

"Flying Dutchman." *Occultopedia, the Occult and Unexplained Encyclopedia*. http://www.occultopedia. com/f/flying_dutchman.htm.

Forde, Matt. "The Mexican Island Haunted by Evil Dolls." *Environmental Graffiti*. Environmental Graffiti, 2010.

Frye, Todd. "The Hope Diamond Curse." *Weird Encyclopedia*, 2007.

"Full Text of 'The Ballads & Songs of Derbyshire. With Illustrative Notes, and Examples of the Original Music, Etc.'" Internet Archive.

Getchell, Susan. "A Doll's Story: Coincidence or Something Else?" *Quesnel Cariboo Observer*. September 2, 1992: A17+.

"Ghost of Bloody Mary." *Religious-information.com*.

"Ghostly Tales and a Graveyard Trail." *Shirley Plantation*.

"The Golden Gate." *Haunted Bay*. http://www.haunted bay.com/features/goldengate.shtml.

"Golden Gate Bridge." *Weird California*. Weird California.

Gottlieb, Matthew. "Aaron Burr's Conspiracy." *The History Channel Club*. June 4, 2009.

Guiley, Rosemary. *The Encyclopedia of Ghosts and Spirits*. New York: Facts on File, 1992.

Hambrick, Judd. Ed. "Aaron Burr's Daughter Disappears: Pirates Suspected." *Southern Memories and Updates*. October 4, 2011. http://southernmemo riesandupdates.com/stories/aaron-burrs-daughter -disappears-pirates-suspected/.

Harrington, Hugh T. "Wayne's Bones." *AmericanRevolution.org*. American Revolution.org.

Hauck, Dennis William. *Haunted Places: The National Directory: A Guidebook to Ghostly Abodes, Sacred Sites, UFO Landings, and Other Supernatural Locations*. New York: Penguin, 1996.

"Haunted Dolls —Paranormal or Just Plain Creepy?" *Weekly Spectre*. May 21, 2010.

"Haunted Items." *Haunted Items*. Mysterious Britain & Ireland. November 12, 2008.

"Hereford Museum Collections." *Herefordshire Museum*. Herefordshire Council.

"History of a Colour: Haint Blue." *Histories of Things to Come.* Histories of Things to Come. September 20, 2011.

"History of the Catacombs of Paris." *Catacombs of Paris Museum.* Catacombes De Paris.

"History of the Hope Diamond." *Smithsonian Education.* Smithsonian Institute.

Holzer, Hans. *Ghosts: True Encounters with the World Beyond.* New York: Black Dog & Leventhal, 1997

"Hope Diamond." *PBS.* PBS.

"How to Protect Against Ghosts." *How to Protect Against Ghosts.* Manzanillo's Best Travel Guide.

"In the Wake of the Zaca." *The Sailing Channel.* 2009.

"Is Belcourt Castle in Rhode Island Haunted?" *The Haunted Hovel.* The Haunted Hovel.

Kaczmarek, Dale. "Eastland Disaster." *Ghost Research Society.* Ghost Research Society, 2011.

Karl, Jason, and Derek Acorah. "The Case of the Haunted Doll." *21st Century Ghosts: Encounters with Ghosts in the New Millennium.* London: New Holland, 2007.

Kelly, John. "'Black Aggie': D.C. Statue Cloaked in Superstition." *Washington Post* (Washington, D.C.). August 18, 2012.

Kennedy, Duncan. "Concealed Shoes: Australian Settlers and an Old Superstition." *BBC News*. BBC, March 16, 2012.

"Lady Lovibond. Goodwin Sands." *Haunted Island*. Haunted Island. December 17, 2010.

Lamkin, Virginia. "The Ghost of Theodosia Burr Alston." *Seeks Ghosts*. Central New Mexico Ghost Investigations. September 27, 2011.

———. "Ghost Ship: Lady Lovibond." *Seeks Ghosts*. Central New Mexico Ghost Investigations, May 29, 2011.

———. "Haunted Electric Chair: Ted Bundy." *Seeks Ghosts*. Central New Mexico Ghost Investigations. March 30, 2012.

———. "Rudolph Valentino's Ghost and Cursed Ring." *Seeks Ghosts*. Central New Mexico Ghost Investigations. September 20, 2011.

———. "Shirley Plantation: The Ghost of Aunt Pratt." *Seeks Ghosts*. Central New Mexico Ghost Investigations. November 21, 2011.

Lechniak-Cumerlato, Stephanie. "Superstitions, Legends, Folklore, and Black Cats." *Haunted Hamilton*.

"Legend of the Screaming Skull." *Screaming Skull*. Real British Ghosts.

Legg, Rodney. "Bettiscombe." *Dorset Life*. Dorset Life. June 2009.

Lewis, Fairweather. "Lady Lovibond." *Fairweather Lewis*. Fairweather Lewis. April 1, 2010.

———. "Valentino's Ring." *Fairweather Lewis*. N.p., September 28, 2010.

"London Bridge—Lake Havasu City." *Haunted Places of Arizona*.

Lorenzi, Rossella. "Roman Curses Appear on Ancient Tablet." *Discovery News*. Discovery. August 21, 2012.

"Mandy." *Quesnel & District Museum and Archives*. Quesnel & District Museum and Archives.

"Mexico's Creepiest Tourist Destination: Island of the Dolls." *Web Urbanist*. WebUrbanist.

Mingus, Jade. "History and Hauntings of The Driskill Hotel." *Kvue.com*. October 30, 2012.

Moran, Mark. "Robert—Key West's Living Doll." *Weird U.S.* New York: Sterling, 2009.

———. "The Two Graves of Mad Anthony Wayne." *Weird U.S.* New York: Sterling, 2009.

"Most Haunted Places in America: Haw Branch Plantation." *Ghost Eyes*. Most Haunted Places in America.

"The Moving Coffins of Barbados." *The Moving Coffins of Barbados*. Slightlywarped.com.

Nickell, Joe. "Another Ghost in the Mirror: Marilyn at the Hollywood Roosevelt?" *Center for Inquiry.* May 31, 2011.

Norman, Michael, and Beth Scott. *Historic Haunted America.* New York: Tor, 2007.

Ogden, Tom. *The Complete Idiot's Guide to Ghosts and Hauntings.* Indianapolis, IN: Alpha, 2004.

———. *Haunted Hollywood: Tinseltown Terrors, Filmdom Phantoms, and Movieland Mayhem.* Guilford, CT: Globe Pequot, 2009.

Okonowicz, Ed. *Haunted Maryland: Ghosts and Strange Phenomena of the Old Line State.* Mechanicsburg, PA: Stackpole, 2007.

Parkinson, Daniel. "Screaming Skulls—An Introduction." *Mysterious Britain & Ireland.*

Parzanese, Joe. "Ships." *Weird California.* New York: Sterling, 2009.

"Phantoms of Old House Woods near Mathews, Virginia." *Mid-Atlantic Hauntings and Ghosts.* Mid-Atlantic Hauntings and Ghosts. November 12, 2011.

Pony. "An Evening at The DrisKILL." *Reviews by Pony.* April 9, 2012.

"The Possessed Doll … Annabell." *Butner Blogspot.* http://butnerblogspot.wordpress.com/2008/10/04/the-possessed-dollannabell/. October 4, 2008.

Powell, Kimberly. "Death & Burial Customs." *About.com Genealogy*. About.com.

Ramsland, Katherine. "Ted Bundy's Ghost." *Psychology Today*. October 27, 2012.

Rebman, Kimberly P. *Haunted Florida: A Guide to the Departed Soul*. Bloomington, IN: AuthorHouse, 2008.

Reilly, Fiona. "Langde: The Protection of Silver." *Life on Nanchang Lu*. Lifeonnanchanglu.com/. April 28, 2011.

Reinbold-Gee, Shannon. "Belcourt Castle." *Real Haunted Houses Belcourt Castle Comments*. Real Haunts.

"Restless Skulls." *Peakland Heritage*. Peakland Heritage.

"Robert the Doll." *Key West Art and Historical Society*. Key West Art and Historical Society.

"Roosevelt Hotel." *Hollywood Haunted House, Roosevelt Hotel, HauntedHouses.com*. HauntedHouses.com.

Rosenberg, Jennifer. "The Curse of the Hope Diamond." 20th Century History. About.com/.

"Rowan." *Controverscial.Com*. http://www.controverscial.com/Rowan.htm.

Savill, Richard. "400-year-old Mummified Cat Found in Walls of Cottage." *The Telegraph*. Telegraph Media Group. April 22, 2009.

"Sawston Hall." *Mysterious Britain & Ireland*. Mysterious Britain & Ireland.

"The Screaming Woman of Haw Branch." *Ghost Stories & Haunted Places*. Hauntedstories.net.

"Secrets of the Smithsonian—History of the Hope Diamond." Smithsonian Education.

Seton, Alexander. "Extract of Manuscript." *Scotsman.com*. Johnston Publishing. April 21, 2005.

"Shoes in the Wall." *Shoes in the Wall*. Wayland Historical Society.

"The Skulls Of Calgarth Hall." *The Skulls Of Calgarth Hall*. Bedlam Library.

Smith, Katherine S. "Don CeSar Hotel Gets a Major Makeover, Name Change." *Tampa Bay Times*. September 17, 2011.

"Star of India." *Star of India*. HauntedHouses.com.

"Star of India." *Haunted Ghost Ship, San Diego*. GoThere Corporation.

Stefko, Jill. "Moving Coffins Cases: Buxhowden & Chase Families' Crypts." *Suite101.com*.

Steiger, Brad. *Real Ghosts, Restless Spirits, and Haunted Places*. Canton, MI: Visible Ink, 2003.

Stoner, Barry. "Hope Diamond." *Treasures of the World*. PBS.

"Tall Ship Review." *Tall Ship Review*. Squidoo.

Taylor, L. B. "Crescent Hotel—Eureka Springs!" *American Hauntings*. Whitechapel Productions Press.

———. "Ghosts of London Bridge in Arizona!" *Ghosts of the Prairie History & Hauntings of America*. Troy Taylor/Ghosts of the Prairie.

———. *Haunted Virginia: Ghosts and Strange Phenomena of the Old Dominion*. Mechanicsburg, PA: Stackpole, 2009.

———. "The Haunts of the Hollywood Sign." *Prairie Ghosts*. Troy Taylor/Ghosts of the Prairie, 2001.

———. "Lizzie Borden: History & Hauntings of This Famous Case." *Lizzie Borden: History & Hauntings of This Famous Case*. Whitechapel Productions Press.

Trott, Tim. "The Mysterious Moving Coffins of Barbados." *Your Paranormal*. January 31, 2009.

"Two Graves of 'Mad Anthony' Wayne." *The New York Times*. July 13, 1902.

"USS *Constellation*." *Historic Ships in Baltimore*. Historicships.org.

"The USS *Hornet* Alameda's Haunted Aircraft Carrier." *Haunted Bay*. Haunted Bay.

"Wayne Buried in Two Places." *Paoli Battlefield*. Independence Hall Association.

Weiser, Kathy. "The Haunted Crescent Hotel in Eureka Springs, Arkansas."*Legends of America*. Legends of America. September 2012.

"The Wilful Skull of Chilton Cantelo." *Ghosts UK*. www.ghosts.org.uk.

"Witch Ball Legends." *Sunny Reflections*. Moonlight Go, LLC.

Young, David. "The Eastland Disaster." *Chicago Tribune*. July 24, 1915.